Daniel Puiboube

The Art of Making

MINIATURE MODELS

Photographs by
Édouard Dejay

Translated by Michael Woosnam-Mills
in collaboration with Gabrielle Merchez

ARCO PUBLISHING COMPANY, INC.
New York

Published 1979 by Arco Publishing Company, Inc.
219 Park Avenue South, New York, N.Y. 10003
Originally published under the title *L'Art de construire des
modèles réduits* by Librairie Hachette, Paris 1977
This English translation © John Bartholomew & Son Limited 1979
Printed in Great Britain

Library of Congress Cataloging in Publication Data

Puiboube, Daniel
  The art of making miniature models.

  1. Miniature craft.   2. Models and modelmaking.
I. Title
TT178.P84   745.59'28   77-27999
ISBN 0-668-04564-7

Contents

Scenery, Decoration and Enhancement of Models

The World of Modelling

To the uninitiated, scale-model making is a pastime that almost belongs with children's games—making a few toys which sometimes even work. But in less than twenty years, scale-model making has become something else completely. Of course aeroplanes and boats still have their aficionados. These two groups of modellers are rather special, being the oldest-established. The fascination of steering and operating machines that one has made with one's own hands is combined with the pleasure of making collector's items, a world in miniature. In this respect, modelling is like collecting lead soldiers. But, with the introduction of injected metals and plastics, the products and processes of modern industry have enhanced more traditional methods and materials. In a quarter of a century, the world of the modelling enthusiast has been transformed from the backroom workshop into mass production.

But what can one make as a scale-model? Answer, just about everything: villages, towns, ports, cars, aeroplanes, tanks. The only limitations are how much money and how much time one can give to the hobby. Mention electric trains, and everyone knows what you mean and, of course, an electric train is an example of a scale-model. Actually though, the world of the electric train is so vast that it deserves a separate book to itself. Even so, model-railway buffs find they have problems in common with other modellers when it comes to the background and the scenery.

Today, whether it's aeroplanes, locomotives, cars, or Napoleon's army, plastic sets the tone. About 80 per cent of all models made are in plastic. Plastic has replaced wood, which is now used only in boats and aeroplanes—and even there, plastics have come in strongly. It is no longer metals such as brass or bronze that give a model authenticity in appearance and weight—although of course one can still find superbly crafted models made to scale and using all available materials.

Modelling for Everyone

This book is intended for everyone. Although we have consulted the most expert craftsmen and model-builders, we have examined the easiest methods, and the models that are easiest to find. We hope to convince even the most sceptical that modelling is an intelligent leisure-time activity, and that it is both educational and more rewarding than many other pastimes.

Modelling is an intelligent occupation because it automatically involves research—historical, technological, geographical. This may not seem very important to start with, but then one becomes increasingly self-disciplined and demanding.

Modelling is educational because it requires the concentration in one small area of all the skills necessary for making something—moulding, masonry, painting and decorating, engineering, woodwork—

all on a tiny scale. Contrary to what you might think, for example, of drawing, you do not need to be particularly talented to be a successful modeller. Patience *is* required, and there are a number of tricks and knacks that must gradually be learned. You can never make a model right first time; it takes practice. But, as you progress, pleasure becomes mixed with pride.

Model making is not particularly expensive. A low-cost model might be put together in one weekend, but by the same token, an expensive model can keep the modeller occupied for several months. And the result? Almost invariably, a collector's item, 100 per cent personalised!

Most of this book deals with plastic models. This is the most widespread form of modelling, and it allows the modeller to climb the ladder of achievement, in the truest sense of the word, to the very top.

Expert modellers will forgive us if we do not provide them with the absolute ultimate in techniques of perfection to enhance their already marvellous collections. We have tried to keep it simple, but without confining ourselves to mere generalities.

Finally, a word on collections. Every modeller is inevitably a collector. That is why we have thought it worthwhile to cover this subject in a special chapter, dealing especially with the transformation or renovation of the toys of yester-year.

The Scale of Scale-models

When one speaks of a model on this or that scale, one is referring to the relationship between the dimensions of the real object and those of the model. It is always a question of linear relationships. In other words, a statue that is really 1m 70cm tall will, on a scale of 1/10, be 1.7m/10 or 0.17m tall, which is 17cm. On a scale of 1/100, the same statue would be only 1.7cm tall. The closer a model is to the real thing, the larger we say the scale is. Thus 1/8 is a larger scale than 1/10. When we are making models of things that are themselves very large (liners, large aeroplanes, towns), we use small scales: 1/700, 1/500, 1/100. This means that the objects themselves are 700, 500, or 100 times bigger.

Over the decades, certain scales have been accepted as standard. Thus the normal scale for electric trains is 1/87. The tracks are 16.5mm wide. This scale is known as HO. The N scale, which is another standard, has tracks that are 9mm wide.

There are some particular scales that have come to be used for certain kinds of models. Thus 1/72 and 1/43 are standard for medium-sized modelling. The scales 1/32 and 1/25 are generally used for medium or large objects (statues, cars, planes).

Very large scales (1/12, 1/10, 1/8) are the special preserve of statues, furniture, cars and interior decor.

Realism and Scale

The larger the scale of a model, the more faithfully must the details reflect the real thing. The smaller the scale, the less distinct relief and other features become. There is often a tendency to cheat and give prominence to certain details while allowing others to disappear. From a distance of one metre, on a 1/10 model, an observer sees the details of roof tiles, or the buttons on a military tunic. It is as if he were 10m away from the real thing. On the other hand if he is looking at a 1/87 model, he cannot see those same details, because it is as though he were 87m away.

Besides variations in size, as the scale alters there are also changes in colour. A bright red at 1/10 becomes a faded red on the same model at 1/100. Material that looks grainy at 1/10 is uniform at 1/100. However, this can lead to a certain monotony in small-scale models, so we cheat by being slightly over-realistic with some aspects, without changing the colours. Stones, plants and metal take on qualities that set the observer's imagination working. That is why the scale-model maker's finished model will always seem more alive than one made by an architect, even if the latter is more delicate or more exact.

Raw Materials and Know-how

Tools, Equipment and Workshop

The Minimum Requirements

Perhaps it is a bit pretentious to talk of a workshop, but frequently the model-maker's chief problem, even more than the necessary skills and handicraft ability, is that of finding space. To begin with, you need a working surface. If it is a household table, it should be easily washable. The next essential is two drawers—one for tools, and the other for modelling accessories. Finally, you need a safe corner out of everyone else's reach for keeping your models in progress. This is the minimum area needed. Ideally, you want a quiet room, well lit, with a desk. We will come back to this point.

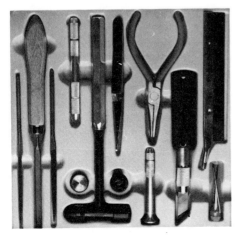

Tools to do everything: Holding and Fixing in Place

The beginner buying his first box of plastic models never thinks to equip himself correctly. The result, assembly and sticking problems. Whether it's aeroplanes or boats, electric trains or dioramas, certain tools immediately seem indispensable—those that help to handle things. The model-maker has only got two hands, but he often needs three or four. When he is assembling parts, his fingers always seem too big or too clumsy. With the right equipment, most of his work will be easier.

Tweezers

To assemble models properly, two types of tweezers are needed: simple tweezers, which allow you to hold and fix in place a delicate object; and reverse tweezers (if you squeeze them they let go, if you relax your grip they close). These tweezers allow a piece to be held in place, leaving the two hands free for other work on the same components.

'Extra Hands'

Certain tools, known as X-tra hands, hold components in place while you work on them. There are two models in the shops, one with one arm and one with two arms. Alligator clips mounted on swivel-joints are supported on a heavy steel base. This arrangement enables you, for instance, to

The minimum tool-kit: files and chisels, flat-saw, cutter, pliers, rivetting hammer and, of course, tweezers.

Tools to do everything: Cutting and Finishing

Whether you are working in wood, in plastic, or in metal, it is essential to have at least a number of basic tools. First of all, there is the model-maker's knife, or cutter. This does the fine work of cutting, scraping and finishing wood or plastic parts. When first equipping yourself, it is a good idea to choose one that consists of a grip with interchangeable blades. You can fit various blades onto this one tool, including a small saw-blade, which comes in handy for wood. For working with uncut wood, a new tool appeared on the market in 1976. This is the rasp-file. This rough-trimming tool saves a lot of time in the early stages.

Above: Screw clamps used to be an essential part of the wood-modeller's tool-kit. Even for plastic modelling, they still have their uses.
Below: Small vice with suction-cap; a simple device for rapid fixing of objects, usable on any flat surface.

solder wires, to glue pieces in mid-air as it were, and to make delicate joints. Alligator clips, such as those used in electrical and radio assembly work, also come in very handy, if only to press together two small parts to be glued.

Small Vices

Even the smallest engineering vice is far too large for the model-maker. You should get either a special vice or, failing that, a vice with a suction-cup: this will remain in place if pressed onto any smooth table-top. It holds pieces in place while you work.

Those who assemble boats and aeroplanes in plastic should add a pair of plastic screw-clamps. These can open to 5.5 or 6cm, which is enough for most occasions.

Abrasives

Rather than wearing out the ends of your fingers trying to get a piece of sandpaper or emery paper into corners, try using an abrasive-holder. You can get sets of three or four differently-shaped holders, flat, V-shaped, and round. This accessory is especially useful for finishing wood, plastic or metal. The simple wooden spindle round which a piece of sandpaper is folded does equally well for papering large surfaces. It is important to have sandpaper always available, and always extra-fine grain.

Here one must do better than just having the right tools—they must be perfect, because whatever the model-maker's speciality—boats, tanks, electric trains—he will have to do a lot of paintwork jobs. Besides the skills and knacks described below, it is essential to be properly equipped.

Paintbrushes

By far the best quality is achieved with English brushes, which can be obtained at modelling shops or graphic-arts stores. They range from 100 calibre to 12 calibre, in 14 sizes. Choose red marten-hair brushes, fine quality, with nickel-plated collars.

There is an exact use for each brush:

00, 0, 1	for precise detailing, e.g. faces, uniforms, engine parts.
2, 3	precise painting of details such as harness and small objects on clear surfaces up to several square centimetres.
4, 5, 6	continuous painting on less important areas needing precision to within not more than 0.5 to 1mm.
7 to 12	for major surface-area painting (i.e. many square centimetres); up to size 7, the features painted may be considered delicate.

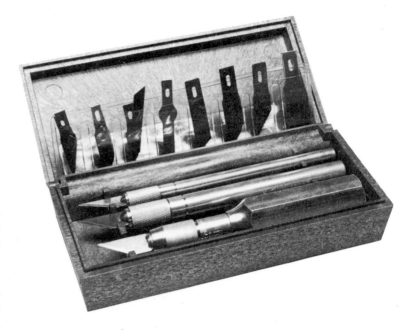

The X-Acto cutting-tool kit. If the uses of some cutters are not immediately obvious, they are still worth having. With them you can do delicate work on cardboard, plastic and wood, and even on leather.

Mixing Bowls and Accessories

The paint to be used on plastic is left in the small pots it comes in, but paints intended for the larger surfaces, applied to wood or paper, are prepared in glass mixing bowls or basins.

When working with hydrocarbon solvent paints, it is a good idea to have a brush-rinser—the kind where the metal collar is gripped in a spring so that only the bristles are dipped in the solvent.

The Drawing Brush

This accessory, also known as a 'Speed-ball', is a spatula and comes in 1/4in and 3/8in sizes (American-made). The uniform width allows the painting of uniform bands and lines on boats, planes and cars. It can also be used in a diorama, for picking out roads and pavement lines.

Spray-can Paints

These allow rapid and easy covering of large surfaces, but we suggest you stock only a small range—about ten different hues, some matt, others gloss. Spray paints are good for undercoats on tanks, cars, planes and trains. The paint is usually sprayed on before the plastic components are detached from the manufacturer's grid-support.

Spray paint can be used on plastic (rigid polystyrene), white metals, and wood. In the case of power models using fuels or high-power solvents, a protective spray fuel-proofer must be applied. This can be applied only onto matt paints. Metallized paint cannot be protected against the effects of fuel.

Thinners and Sundry Constituents

There are one or two more items to be added to the list of basic paintwork equipment, especially for the power-model builder.

Clear seals: These are painted on in the normal way. They help in the contracting and sealing processes in the nylon-skinned balsa-wood of model aeroplanes. You can get reinforced or 'double-clear' paint, but it takes much longer to dry; it should be used only on large models.

Special nitrate seals (colour): These are for painting a second undercoat over a clear base. Obtainable in blue, grey, red, yellow, orange, silver and black.

Sanding-sealing: Treatment of aeroplane or boat balsa-wood before application of enamel paint or varnish.

Thinners: Any number of these are available in the shops. They are used to dilute all cellulose-base paints.

The Model-maker's Paint-spray Gun

This is really a precision instrument, and here is how it works. The gun itself screws onto a small paint pot. A liquid-gas bottle provides the propellant. The gun has a double control, governing air and paint flow. Since the grain and density of the paint can be varied, a great many types of finish are possible.

Air Brushes

These permit very subtle variations in your painting, such as camouflage effects, mist, dirt and mud. The ones you can buy have 0.2 or 0.3mm tips. You can use them with water-colours or with cellulose-alcohol varnishes. For correct use of the air brush, the paint must be well thinned and completely smooth. The air brush is connected to a small compressor. (Some can run off a gas bottle). An air brush is really like a precision paint-spray gun.

Drawing Pens

Nib thicknesses range from 0.2 to 1.2mm. They are sold in sets (7 different nibs) and used with special black ink. You can use very diluted paint instead, but only for a few moments, and the pen and nib must be thoroughly rinsed at once afterwards. Ideal for all drawing of fine lines. (On 1/87, or HO locomotives, for example, or on cars and planes at 1/72). The 0.2 and 0.4 nibs are suitable for the finer details, and must be used only with black ink. The drawing pen allows the beginner to draw fine, regular lines, which is difficult to do with a brush.

Paints

There is a huge variety of paints available to the model-maker. These often differ according to the material they are intended for, but the same paint or varnish can be used on different materials, so we list them here by type of paint, with recommendations as to their various uses.

Poster paints: These are water-based paints, obtainable from artists' supply shops. Most brands come in about thirty colours, all of which can be mixed with each other in any combination. These oily looking paints are suitable for use on plywood, cardboard, expanded polystyrene, drawing paper, wood veneers and all kinds of decorative mouldings. Poster paints can

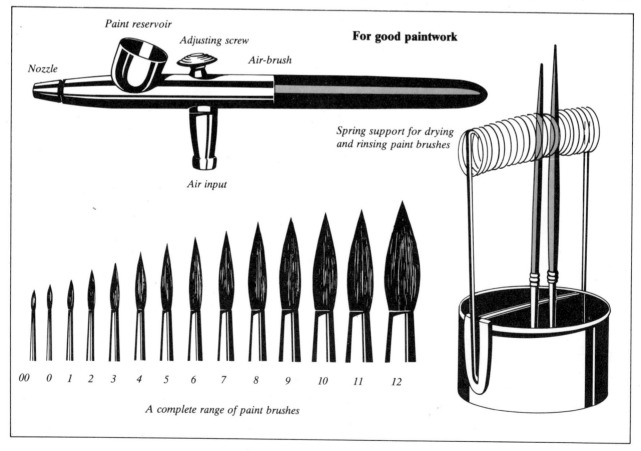

Nozzle

Paint reservoir

Adjusting screw

Air-brush

For good paintwork

Air input

Spring support for drying and rinsing paint brushes

00 0 1 2 3 4 5 6 7 8 9 10 11 12

A complete range of paint brushes

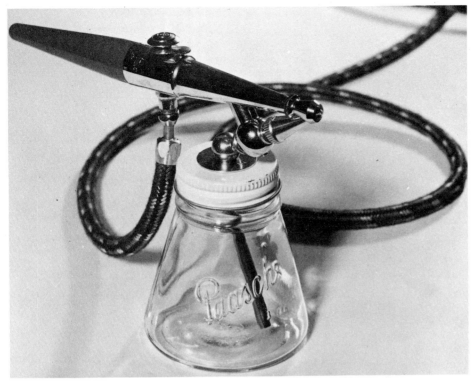

The air-brush; universally useful. Propulsion is provided by a pressurized liquid-gas container.

be applied with a miniature roller or any brush between sizes 2 and 12.

It should be noted that modellers' and artists' suppliers also carry professional acrylic poster paints. These can be used on plastic without contracting or cracking. They can also be used on cellulose acetate (the transparent parts of plastic models). They come in a range of about fifty colours.

Model-maker's paints: These are the model-maker's basic ingredient. They come in small 15ml pots. They come in various ranges—standard colours, matt and gloss—used for all non-military models, of individual or standard design. General all-purpose paints, including 'metal' shades (gold, silver, red, green, brown, etc.).

High-fidelity paints: Specially developed for the painting of specialized models. The range includes the colours used by the Royal Air Force, the U.S. Army and the Wehrmacht. They are labelled 'Authentic Colour', and have interesting technical properties: without any loss of opacity, the extreme thinness of the dried paint means there is no blurring of fine detail on the model. This paint dries without brush marks. It comes in the following high-fidelity colours: R.A.F., Italian Army (1939–45), Russian Army (1939–45),

armoured vehicles (1945–70), uniforms (1939–45), historical British uniforms, French Air Force (1939–40 and present-day). There are also special ranges for model railway enthusiasts.

Precision Tools for Metal-working

The model-maker uses, in miniature, the same tools that are found in a regular workshop. Some are genuinely useful, while others are mere gadgets.

Electric drill: Various battery-operated models are available from modellers' suppliers. The most interesting feature of these is the chuck, which permits the drilling of very small holes. Carbon bits range in size from 1/80 to 1/45in. Precision bits ranging from ½mm to 2mm are also available. The electric drill can also take brushes and cutters, on a stand or hand-held. Always remember that to work metal correctly you must choose the correct rotation speed. Thus a drill turned by hand is quite unsuitable. Versatility is the keynote: a metal-working drill performs equally well on wood and on plastic. There are some brands of drill that can be used as a wood or metal lathe, in which case they can be plugged into the mains.

Soldering iron: Obtainable from any electrical shop. Indispensable for lighting connections, assembling of electric motors—or for tin-soldering and brazing. We suggest that a soldering gun is rather more practical. They come nowadays in 220-volt models, running at 90 to 100 watts. They reach the desired temperature immediately. The fine soldering iron, available from modellers' suppliers, can be used not only for soldering, but also for cutting: aluminium or plastic, for example, can be melted, and the narrow-pointed tip can be used like a pencil.

Certain equipment and materials that have more specialized uses, or are of interest only to a particular group of model-makers, are explained later on in this book.

The mini-drill is not just a gadget. It can run on mains or batteries. With its stand and multiple attachments, it can if necessary be used as a slotting or milling machine.

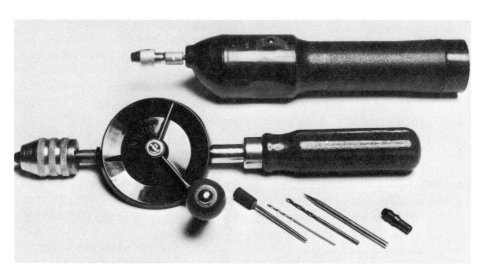

Other drilling tools: the hand-brace and hand-drill. The former is suitable for wood, while the latter permits engraving and finishing with the appropriate attachments.

16

The Model-Maker's Materials

We have just been examining the various basic tools and equipment that the model-maker will need. Here now is a group of materials, sundry products and tools that, while not specifically designed for the model-maker, are nevertheless worth getting to know because they can be extremely useful.

Model-Making Products

It is worth learning the possibilities of these, used as they are by professionals and experts. Some are expensive, others economical.

Expanded Polystyrene

This material, used nowadays for all kinds of packaging, is worth saving whenever possible. It is unfortunately not impervious to glues and solvents. It is light and easy to work. It can be cut either with an electric cutter or with a very fine-toothed saw. Polystyrene is ideal for any scale greater than 1/43. It enables you to construct walls and facades of buildings. Light even when bulky, it is always easy to work.

The first piece of advice for a model-maker should be: always save polystyrene packing. For those who do not have a fine-toothed jigsaw, polystyrene can be worked with a saw-blade, a jeweller's file, or a cross-cut wire-saw, or polystyrene can be shaped with a small-bladed knife. Expanded polystyrene can also be purchased as draught-excluding strips, 0.5, 0.8, 1 and 2cm wide.

Polystyrene's chief rival is cork, which is more elegant for constructing walls and buildings. Cork is more elastic, less rigid when upright, and can be used as it is, unprocessed. Polystyrene, on the other hand, can be painted.

Solder also comes miniaturized. Pictured here, the miniaturized oxidizing burner for delicate work in metal. Its thermal capacities are in no way inferior to those of the full-size burner. Particularly useful for the model railway enthusiast, and also for constructing aeroplanes and boats built of metal.

The Use of Plaster and Plastics

Plaster was the first material that model-makers used with wood, and for a long time has been the typical medium. By 'plastics' we mean those materials besides kaolinite and gypsum that are cellulose-based or contain vinyl additives.

Modelling plaster (or Plaster of Paris) is easily obtained. It is prepared by sprinkling the dry plaster into a bowl or other receptacle containing water. The resulting paste will look slightly oily as the plaster thoroughly absorbs the water, but it will remain white in colour. There are two basic types of plaster to use: rapid-setting and slow-setting. The choice is determined by the model-maker's particular needs. While plaster permits the construction, for example, of detailed countryside, its drawback is that it is very heavy. So it is best used in thin layers supported by something else (see the chapter on the making of scenery etc.). Used flat, plaster can be used to make paving, walls and anything that is supposed to look like masonry of any kind. It is one of the model-maker's most economical materials, but has the disadvantage of setting too rapidly.

Tools for Working Plaster

The model-maker who wants to build a lot of scenery around his models will need some sculpting chisels. These tools are to plaster what the X-Acto tools are to wood. They come pointed, chamfered, or curved, for etching and contouring work.

Jointers are for use on both plaster and modelling clays. They are small wires of various shapes, attached to handles. They can do, on plaster, what scrapers, rasps and planes can do on wood.

Besides plaster, there are a number of brand-name products that can be used as basic material, Faserit, for example. Faserit is a white powder that comes in flake form, consisting in fact of cellulose fibres. Mixed with water, it hardens in twenty-four hours. Faserit permits the moulding of elegant relief-work in large-scale models. But beware: Faserit can be used only if it is well supported. Faserit mouldings can, when dry, be painted in water colours, or with acrylic and vinyl paints.

There are various modelling clays available in 500 gram packets that can be used just like plaster. They are easy to work, and can also be used to make impressions, as one might do with wax. Modelling clays usually come in the basic colours required for buildings and countryside: grey, white, yellow and ochre.

Liquid Form-paint

This is the name of a widely available product, that consists of either transparent or coloured cellulose. It is simple to use, and is good for such things as windscreens, glass roofs, windows, domes, military uniforms, tents, tarpaulins etc. It is used as follows: a transparent mould is made from suitably shaped metal or copper wire netting. (Liquid form-paint comes in the following colours: red, emerald green, blue, brown, neutral, purple, white and orange). The wire is dipped into a bowl containing liquid form-paint, then taken out and shaken to remove the surplus. To dry (which takes 5 minutes), the mould should be placed on a piece of expanded polystyrene. Liquid form-paint has two major disadvantages: it is not very long-lasting, and it is very expensive.

Moulding Equipment

You have a model of a lamp, or a building, or some other scale-model that you would like to make several copies of. How can you do it? You can make a mould yourself, out of elastomer-silicone.

This is actually various viscous liquids which, when combined with the appropriate catalyst at room temperature, turn into solids with the texture of rubber and the general properties of silicone products, which means there is no 'unmoulding' procedure. Known in the trade as R.T.V., elastomer-silicone permits the making of supple moulds, resistant to chemical agents, able to withstand temperatures up to 250 °C. The moulds can be used for plaster, for polyester, or for polyurethane foam, and will give faithful reproduction. For example, starting from a model in mere plastic, you can make a building out of concrete or plaster using an R.T.V. mould. R.T.V. is also good for making moulds of such things as wood, gravel, wire netting, etc., which would be hard to reproduce accurately by hand.

Different uses for different materials

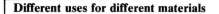

1 — The use of expanded polystyrene

Gullies, slopes, building foundations

Ruins, blind wall sections

2 — The use of plastic wood

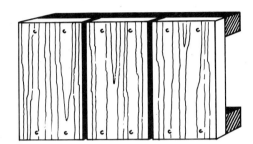

Assembly before treatment

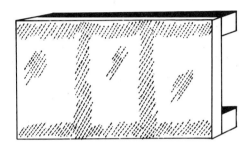

After sealing with plastic wood, the component is ready for polishing

3 — The use of polyurethane foam

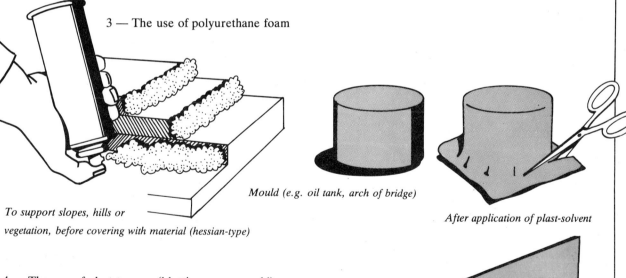

To support slopes, hills or vegetation, before covering with material (hessian-type)

Mould (e.g. oil tank, arch of bridge)

After application of plast-solvent

4 — The use of plast-temper (blotting-paper mould)

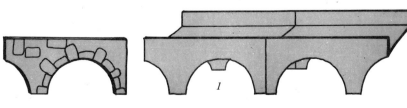

Three ready-to-paint copies made from one original (number 1)

The Use of Plastic Mould-mountings

This is a rather special procedure. Epoxy resins, with the addition of a plastifying agent, can be used to encase certain objects in a matrix. Toy soldiers, cars or other small models could be thus immersed in a plastic block. Epoxy resins are available as a viscous liquid of 1.3 density. They can last for a year at 20 °C. The liquid is spread over the object to be mould-mounted. Epoxys are odourless and have a low exothermic reaction, which means they flow efficiently. The manufacturers give very precise details—but beware: epoxys do not keep for long, so you should use only the amount required for each operation.

Polyester Compounds

These multi-purpose materials have all the usual qualities of such compounds—malleability and suppleness. Polyester compounds can, with the help of an additive, be made to stick to metal, stone, wood, and even polyester if the surface has been roughened. They harden without shrinking and can be worked with any ordinary tool. The advantages are obvious. A plastic model can be partially altered by the addition of polyester-compound parts (for example lengthening the nose of an aeroplane or altering a ship's funnel). Polyester compounds are better known under their brand names.

Plastic Wood

Used by cabinet-makers for a quarter of a century, 'plastic wood' is also used by professional model-makers. There are various brand names. It comes either as a ready-to-use paste, like a cement, or in a block from which you break off the required amount and dissolve in solvent. Synthetic wood also comes as an oily paste, which can be worked with a spatula or a knife. Drying and hardening are rapid. Plastic wood can be used to correct small errors or minor damage. For scenery, it is useful in balsa-wood construction where relief moulding is not suitable—building-facades, porches, monumental arches, etc. By dipping a brush into the solvent and applying it to the plastic wood already in place, satisfying results can be achieved.

Plastic Metal

This is a resin to which is added a metallic pigment, which is absorbed. The end result looks like metal. Thus an image of the real appearance of pewter, bronze, copper, brass or iron is reproduced in the material itself. Ethyl acetate can be used on the surface to create a patina of age. Depending how much solvent is used, you get either a viscous fluid or a paste. In the first case, the plastic metal should be applied in thin layers with a spatula or a brush. A spray gun can also be used, for thinner application. There are various brand names of plastic metal. It is particularly useful for making alterations to large components—engines, aeroplanes, vehicle chassis etc., and it is cheaper than buying the new parts.

Polyurethane Foam in Aerosol Cans

A relatively new product, this is usually sold as a gasket or washer sealant. It comes in 1-kilo cans, giving about 25 to 30 litres of foam. The can must be shaken first, just like shaving-cream. The cooler and more humid it is, the more readily the foam will flow. Ideal working temperature is 20−25 °C. The foam is very light and will stick to anything—cloth, wood, hard plastic. It enables you to construct beadings and copings which are essential for background scenery in relief. You can use it on kraft paper or on hessian. The foam never totally solidifies, which means you can stick things into it, such as trees, posts, fencing—while any cracks can be smoothed over with cellulose paste.

The can must be shaken vigorously before the nozzle is depressed. The foam will then flow regularly. Do not apply it too thickly. It is best to use up all the foam on the same day. Apart from its use in background scenery, the foam's lightness means it can also be used as a filler, or even as an isolating substance in some models. It is important to remove foam from the hands after use before it solidifies and sticks—this should always be done within five minutes.

The Use of Sealants and Other Protective Coatings

We have just been talking about the use of plaster and other more recently developed materials, such as sealants etc. It is worth noting that do-it-yourself shops stock plugging and filling seals and fillers, and that they are extremely useful. The ones that come as powder for you to prepare yourself are much cheaper than those sold in tubes; the fact that tubes are ready for instant use is hardly a decisive factor for the model-maker. At no great expense these seals and fillers can be used to surface roads, buildings, hills, walls etc., on small-scale and larger-scale models. The powder is mixed with water and spread with a wooden or metal spatula. Because it is so malleable, you can apply it in very thin layers. There is one particular model making product which gives excellent results when used with a spatula, and that is Corenan. Corenan is a fibrous compound, rather like the one sometimes used to make fibre pegs or posts. When cut with a tool, Corenan breaks cleanly without flaking. Thus it can be used to alter scenery or countryside, both during and after construction.

Corasphalt is particularly useful for making masonry or paving on a large-scale model, say anything bigger than 1/72 or 1/43. Corasphalt can be made to look exactly like masonry. It can be worked with a spatula or with an X-Acto tool. Corasphalt has one big advantage over plaster, in that it sticks to wood.

Using 'Tape' and 'Letraset' Patterns and Screens

Like most adhesive tapes, Normatape comes on spools 0.4 to 4.76mm. The tape is laid from left to right or from right to left, as convenient. With the thinner tape, unroll easily-held lengths of 4 to 5cm before applying it to the model. With the thicker tape, lengths of 10cm are suitable. Before sticking the tape in place, trace its exact positioning. Once the tape is unrolled it must be applied in a single stroke, gently but firmly, to avoid the appearance of creases.

Guide patterns that represent, in black, the shape of things like wood, stone or tiles, can be applied to drawing paper or to a coloured surface. The pattern may be self-sticking, or of the transfer type. The self-sticking kind can be cut to the dimensions desired with a knife or with scissors; the sticking is best done with a wooden spatula or the back of a penknife

blade. You can get patterns in any matt colour as well, and on certain surfaces they will do instead of painting. They cut and adhere just like the other kind. You should follow the same procedures as for wall papering. Brush from top to bottom and from right to left to avoid wrinkles.

The transfer guide pattern, which comes on a wax paper backing, adheres by simply being pressed. Beware! the results don't always live up to your expectations! But they can be quite useful for lettering, and for information and road signs.

Things seem easier for the beginner when he is equipped with the correct basic tools, and when he has an idea of the variety of materials available.

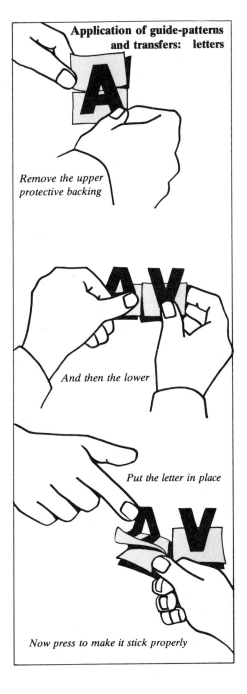

Application of guide-patterns and transfers: letters

Remove the upper protective backing

And then the lower

Put the letter in place

Now press to make it stick properly

Reproduction Without Using Moulds

With certain models, and especially with dioramas, you may want to reproduce the same thing a number of times (building-facades, pavements, balconies, walls) or for a considerable distance, starting off with one small section or model. Rather than making a mould and pouring, you can use a material called Plasttemper. It is a bit like thick blotting paper and comes in rolls 90cm to 1m wide. It is soaked in special solvent (Plastsolvent), and then wrapped around the object you want to reproduce. Leave it to set for about half an hour. It will be hard in thirty minutes. Once hardened, it can be glued, sawn or planed. It can be painted in water-colours, in vinyl-based or in glycerophtalic paints. It is especially useful for scenery—if, for example, you wanted to show two scenes happening in the same place but at different times in history.

The Correct Use of Adhesives

There is no one tube of glue that will do for all modelling jobs. Each technical category has its own particular use.

Rapid setting vinyl glues: Sold in applicator tubes. May be used on cardboard, material, paper or wood. Light pressure ensures setting.

Special plastic glues: Almost exclusively for use on plastic models, although they can stick other substances too. The best brands are non-drip, they do not harden in the tube and are not too runny. (Some that are not at all runny have a tendency to shrivel up into a stalactite at the end of the tube).

Expanded polystyrene glues: Fluid or viscous, these permit the glueing of expanded polystyrene to itself, or to wood, cardboard or metal.

Balsa glues: Particularly useful for glueing balsa-wood where other wood glues will not do, due to particularly good contact and absorptive qualities. Primarily for use in glueing wood and fibreboards; can also be used with earthenware.

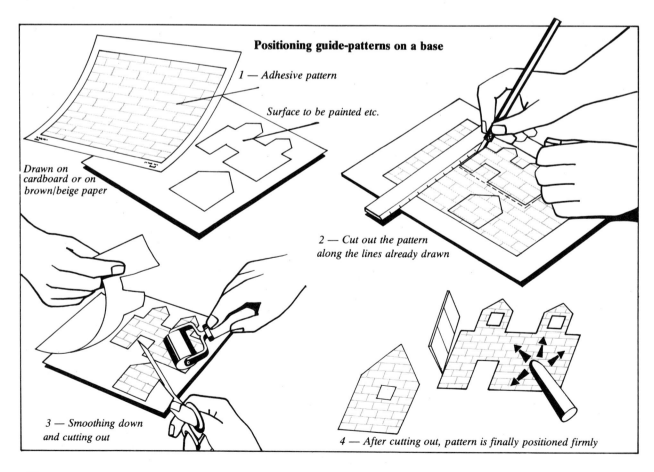

Positioning guide-patterns on a base

1 — Adhesive pattern

Surface to be painted etc.

Drawn on cardboard or on brown/beige paper

2 — Cut out the pattern along the lines already drawn

3 — Smoothing down and cutting out

4 — After cutting out, pattern is finally positioned firmly

Two-component glues: These create a pliable film, permitting glueing of wood, glass (ideal for making windows), and nearly all plastics. Resistant to boiling water. Drying time: overnight.

Cyanolite: This new glue is ideal for assembling all plastic models as it takes only a few seconds to harden.

Special glue for use with altuglass and plexiglass: These glues are dangerous and should be used with care. Used for perspex, altuglass and plexiglass. Handy for the modeller who makes his own windows. (These glues are dichlorethane-based). Altufix, which acts as a binding agent on methylmetacrylate, does the same job.

PVC glues: Rather like the old-fashioned 'solutions'. Good for glueing plastics, or for fixing PVC to bakelite, polystyrene and cellulose acetate.

Wood and Metal

To the model-maker, wood and metal are the materials that he will use to complement and to individualize the basic models which he can purchase. It is true that, generally speaking, the model-maker uses wood in much the same way as a carpenter. But the volumes and areas involved, and the precision of the work, demand a care and a skill that are often unknown to the average handyman.

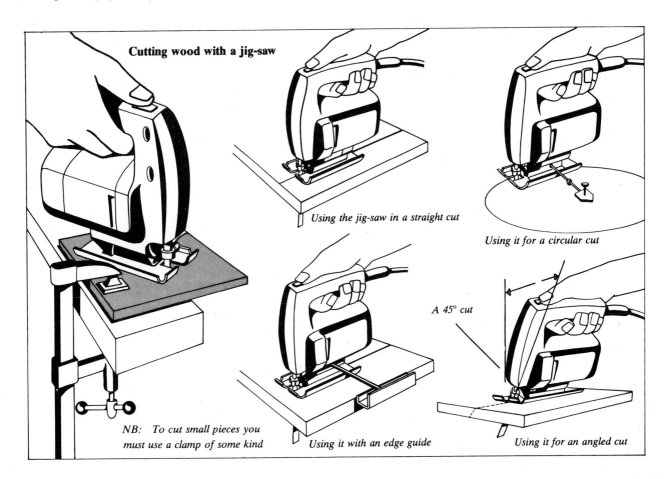

Cutting wood with a jig-saw

Using the jig-saw in a straight cut

Using it for a circular cut

A 45° cut

NB: To cut small pieces you must use a clamp of some kind

Using it with an edge guide

Using it for an angled cut

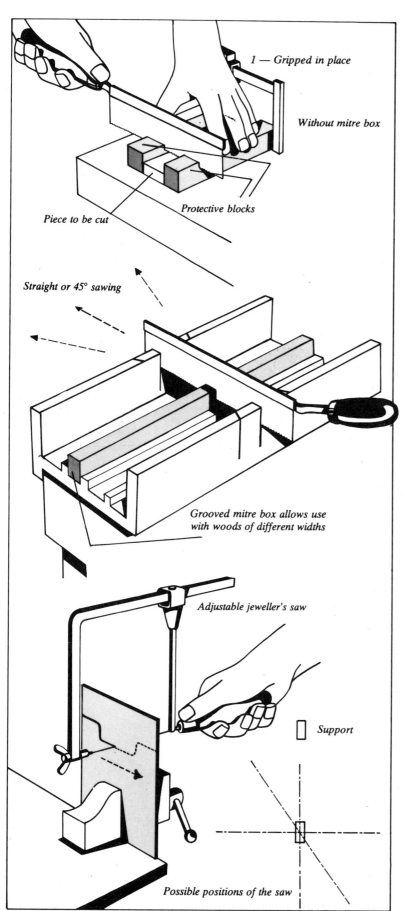

1 — Gripped in place

Without mitre box

Piece to be cut

Protective blocks

Straight or 45° sawing

Grooved mitre box allows use
with woods of different widths

Adjustable jeweller's saw

Support

Possible positions of the saw

Working in Wood

Most of the preparatory work is done with the standard drill and jigsaw. With its regular bits and heads, the drill is used basically just for the largest pieces of scenery or model railway components. The jigsaw, however, is more versatile in preparation. Choice of blade depends on the material to be worked. Manufacturers advise as follows:

On white wood and hard: Fine-toothed blades or wider-toothed, depending on the thickness to be cut.

On very soft metal (aluminium): Use very sharp-toothed blades.

On wood fibre board: Choose a fine-toothed saw, which may also be used on 6mm cardboard.

On non-ferrous metals: Use a fine-toothed saw, set closer together than for aluminium.

Note how saws are fitted together. Not all jigsaws have a standard attachment system.

Know How to Cut Correctly

Cutting wood, and especially plywood, is the one model-making activity that compares most nearly with do-it-yourself work. All the saws have at least two speeds. So on any one wood you can cut roughly and quickly, or slowly and more finely. With soft wood, the quickest cut should usually be selected. If the blade used is not the right one, it will break or cause vibrations. A wrongly-chosen speed will make the saw jump or stop altogether, 'skidding' in its tracks. The saw must always be held at a constant angle to the wood, which must itself be quite stable and unable to slip, so no unwanted vibrations will occur. For steeled metals, select a speed of 1,500 cuts per minute. For wood, work at 3,000.

Working with the Standard Drill

By the standard drill, we mean the traditional handyman's tool. It is a good tool because of its various changeable heads.

Particularly valuable are:

The flat grooving cutter: This gives long narrow or rectangular grooves in supporting struts (ideal for scenery or windows, for example).

Grinding cutters: A number of small cone-shaped, cylindrical, or spherical grinders facilitating work on wood or other substances. They attach like bits and permit incision work.

Drum rasps: Rough-trimming tools which enable rapid cutting along the edge of a piece of wood held securely in a vice.

How to Drill Metal

Very small pieces which may be difficult to hold properly in a vice can be held in pliers in the left-hand; then the pliers are themselves put into a corner of a vice which is tightened to prevent any chance of slipping. The position of the hole should be marked with a small pointed object. A piece of wood should be placed behind the metal to help prevent any bending of the metal as the bit emerges.

Buffing

This is most often done by hand, but where necessary, a vibrating buffer can be used, usually known as a rotating polisher. Rough-polishing is done with No.1 paper (50 grain), and then you change down to 0 or 2/0 paper (80 to 100 grain). Finishing is done with 6/0 paper (220 grain). For tin-foil and metal-foils that may be used, a

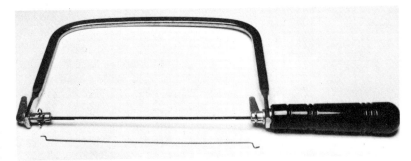

corundum abrasive should be used, 40 to 60 grain and then 100 grain. To buff models made out of plaster, concrete or hydrozell, a 100 grain carborundum abrasive should be used. In all cases, there are three basic steps to follow: rough-polishing, grinding, and final polishing. The model-maker must choose between the various sanding cloths and papers:

Aluminium oxide: For plaster, plastic, wood, and all other materials.

Glass paper (sandpaper): Only for plaster, fibreboards and plastics.

Working with 'Mini-tools'

The mini-drill, battery or mains operated, allows very minute work in metal, wood or plastic. For best effect, it must be used very carefully and at high speed. When working with a mini-drill, we recommend a magnifying glass, a drill mount, and a special vice. Preparation of components before drilling, grinding or polishing is even more important than the operations themselves. Not a single false move—otherwise a tool will break.

Above: The jeweller's saw, extra-fine, handily mounted, comes with many different blades suitable for cutting metal and polystyrene.

Opposite: Brushes and polishers, bits and braces extend the use of the electric drill, and make for clean work on metal or plastic alike.

This kind of micro-tool can be used on plastic or wooden models and especially on metal. Some brands of ordinary drill come with special model-making adaptors that allow the drill to be mounted on a stand. A flexible lead allows the work to proceed without fear of tool-slip. Finally, we should point out that there are available special heads and bits for brass and plastic in standard sizes. For working in very small dimensions (1/2 to 1/8mm), the bits to use are those normally used in the making of watches and jewellery.

Use of the Pyrograph

This is a tool with a tip that heats up. It permits close work on substances whose melting point is, in general, not very high. It can be used on wood or plastic. It works like a miniature soldering-iron. The extremely delicate heated tip oxydizes the plastic, wood, or low-melting metal that it touches. As with most things in model-making, a few experiments should be made with different substances before attempting the job-in-hand. The pyrograph is a useful tool for the model-maker, for making grooves or drilling, and for hollowing out. The tips are interchangeable, allowing holes of varying depths to be made. Among all the specialized tools you can buy, we recommend this one especially for the model-maker interested in making model figures or working in wood. The pyrograph is particularly good for micro-engraving on wood.

Working with Hand Tools

The tools for working on sheets of plywood, or on blocks and pieces of wood, are the same as for regular carpentry. The most important are wood chisels, a plane, a keyhole saw, and a regular saw. It is usually best to do the basic work with portable electric tools and to finish off with micro-tools.

Sawing: A small hand-saw does all cutting of small and large pieces. The very fine-bladed keyhole saw makes openings and small cuts. It can be used for inserting into holes already drilled. It can be replaced by a jigsaw.

Planing: Plane blades must always be well sharpened. The blade should never project more than 1mm below the foot. Sharpening is necessarily frequent, and must always be done on a whetstone, not a grindstone.

Chiselling: You should have only sculptor's chisels, fine enough to allow precision work. The finest carpentry chisel measures 4mm.

Chamfering: A chamfer is much the same as a spokeshave. It is used for rounding off and bevelling.

Assembly

We will not go into the traditional carpenter's methods of joining and fixing, because they do not apply to model-making. However, the glueing procedure is exactly the same. There are basically

Upright position

Section of hole after drilling

Trimming with triangular file

Tweezers

Block

Precise drilling

Guide

Piece to be drilled

Block

two kinds of glue that can be used: synthetic resins especially for wood, and vinyl glues which have the advantage is being able to stick together pieces of wood, cardboard, paper and material. Glueing is often helped by the use of screws and clamps.

Working in Metal

Scale-model Soldering

Soldering is only used for little ancillary jobs in background scenery, but do not hesitate. There is a distinction, in precision work soldering, between soft or tin solder, and hard solder or brazing. In both kinds of soldering, the 'adhesive' used is a metal with a relatively low melting point (250 °C).

Soft soldering (tinning): This is very popular for model railways, but can also be used to join pieces of metal in a number of stationary or mobile constructions—bridges, boats, cars, etc. Soft soldering can join together pieces of copper, steel, lead, zinc and alloys. For precise soldering, you need a small vice, or pairs of alligator clips which will hold the parts or the wires to be joined (or, better, an X-tra hand vice). This leaves both hands free. The best tool is a soldering iron or a soldering gun.

—If you are soldering ferrous metal (steel) you will also need 'killed spirits' (zinc chloride).
—When soldering copper, you will need some soldering flux.
—And for soldering lead, stearin is required.

Each of these three substances acts as a preliminary stripping agent. The procedure is the same in all cases: scrape the pieces to be soldered with a knife, then with emery paper. All greasy substance should be removed with petrol or trichloroethylene. (NB: take the normal precautions against fire hazard).

You can tell when the iron is hot by the characteristic smell of ozone that it gives off. Apply it to one of the pieces to be soldered: this will become heated. Now introduce the solder, held in the left-hand.

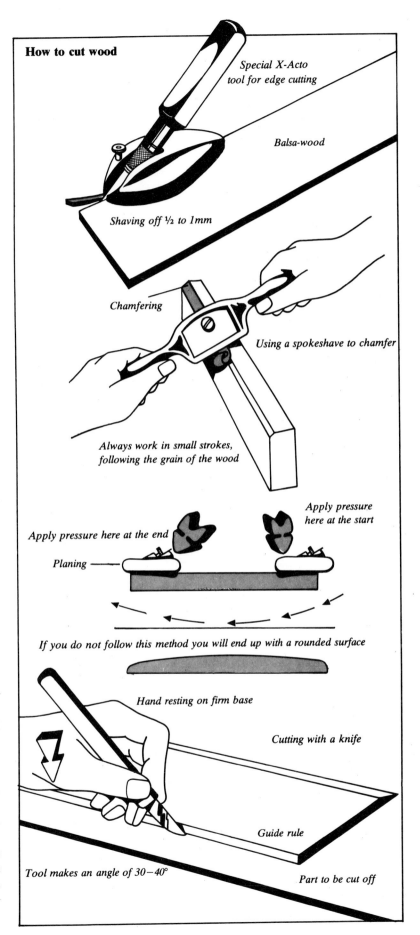

How to cut wood

Special X-Acto tool for edge cutting

Balsa-wood

Shaving off ½ to 1mm

Chamfering

Using a spokeshave to chamfer

Always work in small strokes, following the grain of the wood

Apply pressure here at the start

Apply pressure here at the end

Planing

If you do not follow this method you will end up with a rounded surface

Hand resting on firm base

Cutting with a knife

Guide rule

Tool makes an angle of 30—40°

Part to be cut off

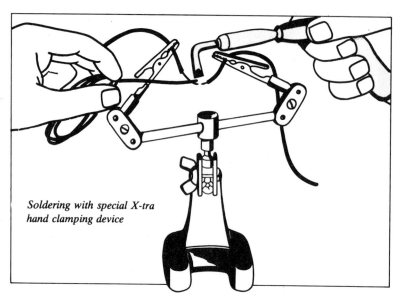

Soldering with special X-tra hand clamping device

immediately used to remove excess solder and to flatten any irregularities. The actual joining of the components is brought about by simultaneously heating them, making the solder melt.

Brazing: In brazing, the joining agent is silver. Brazing is both difficult and expensive. However, there are those who nevertheless swear by it. The components to be joined are cleaned and placed on a non-inflammable surface, such as bricks, tiles, or asbestos. They are held in place with metal blocks or fireproof bricks. They are then sprinkled with borax powder or a similar 'flux', and heated with a blow-lamp. When the components are red-hot, the lamp is removed and the brazing alloy applied immediately. This melts and makes the join.

Making Miniature Electrical Connections etc.

In principle there is nothing difficult about making electrical connections on models. If you can solder a joint, all will be well. Connecting blocks cannot usually be used because they are too big for models. Wires must generally be twisted (or better, spliced) together.

Joining Two Wires

Splicing two wires together means stripping a few millimetres at the end of each. The exposed wires are then twisted round each other, one going to the right and the other to the left. Once the wires are wound together, place a drop of solder on the join. A drop of wax or a drop of gutta-percha will act as an insulator to avoid current-leakage. With scale-models there is no other risk, as they run at 3, 6 or 9 volts.

For all other connections to do with lighting, motors, and other electrical accessories, manufacturers give precise directions.

It will melt at once, making a shiny round globule. Remove the iron immediately. If the solder is uneven, it can be smoothed out by brushing the iron gently along the lines of the pieces being soldered. For a solder to hold properly, the pieces must be held exactly in position throughout the operation.

The preliminary stripping and degreasing mentioned above is essential for the correct soldering of all model components made of tin, aluminium, zinc, or lead. Afterwards, they should be wiped with hydrochloric acid applied with a cloth held in pliers. Try to avoid heating the components themselves too much, so as not to alter their shape.

Tinning: This is a particular tin-soldering process, useful for those who want to make their own components, such as locomotive boilers and car bodywork. The object is to ensure a firm solder with only a thin layer. After cleaning, the two components are heated with a portable welding torch or blow-lamp. A drop of solder is applied, which melts at once and makes the surface shiny. A piece of cotton waste is then

Polystyrene, Paper and Cardboard

We have seen above how to assemble models, from rough putting-together to finishing-off. There are some more advanced techniques that will make them even better. Let us now find out how they can be transformed with the help of modern materials like polystyrene. (See the technical glossary at the end of the book for the various forms in which this material is available).

Working Polystyrene

Whether you are making a model of a boat, a plane, or some other vehicle, polystyrene is a basic material. With it you can make all kinds of modifications and transformations to standard models. It is the number one substance for repairs to cars, tanks, rolling-stock. Working it is somewhat different from working wood. Polystyrene is the essential material used in any major model adaptation.

Cutting

A soft-leaded pencil and a ruler are used to draw lines on polystyrene. Before cutting, score the pencil lines with an X-Acto knife. Two or three scorings will make guidelines for cutting. With a thick piece of polystyrene, do the same thing on the other side. A clean break can then be made with the help of double clamps.

After cutting, polishing is frequently necessary. If it is a curved cut, you should use a cardboard template. The first scoring should be done with a triangular-headed stylus—this will be less likely to slip than a normal blade.

Punching Out Shapes

Rather than actually slicing, or boring holes, with regular tools, it is quite simple to use a heated copper wire of the desired dimension. For example, holes for handles, or supports, or steps, can be heat-bored. Any unwanted rim which appears on the edge of a hole after boring can be eliminated with a cutter or a file.

A miniature drill gives the same result, and it can also be used to make slits for air-vents, hatches, etc.

Cutting Out

Using a piece of polystyrene, you cannot cut out any very complicated shapes. On the other hand, an L-shaped fold can be made quite easily. Score the line of the fold with your cutter and then hold it over a spirit lamp (preferably with a non-carbon flame). Move the flame around and the polystyrene will soften. Bend it into the shape desired. Next place it between brackets and ensure it is in the correct right-angle position. The polystyrene will be hard again in two or three minutes.

When L- or U-shapes or bends are made, weak points may appear in the polystyrene. These 'stretch-marks' can be hidden with Body Putty spread by hand. Once it is dry, simply polish up the area it covers. In subsequent chapters we shall examine the many possibilities of polystyrene, techniques varying with the type of construction.

What can be made with Polystyrene?

Used in model-making, polystyrene (which is shockproof) can represent solid metal (gun-turrets, tank bodies), stonework (walls, bridge supports), buildings and roofs, or support-structures to take other more fragile components.

Working Paper and Cardboard

Thin cardboard and drawing paper are extremely important to the model-maker. Because they are so thin (from a few tenths of a millimetre to 1mm), they are a good size for most flat surfaces, such as partitions, planking, tiles and small sections. The one drawback is obviously lack of rigidity. $223g/m^2$ weight paper can only be used in pieces up to 5 by 10cm without backing to reinforce it.

Tracing

The advantage of drawing paper is that it allows all kinds of complicated tracing with drawing pen and compass. It can be coloured, and serves as a base for relief-work. A flat tracing can either be left as it is, or folded over for extra thickness to give a small additional relief effect.

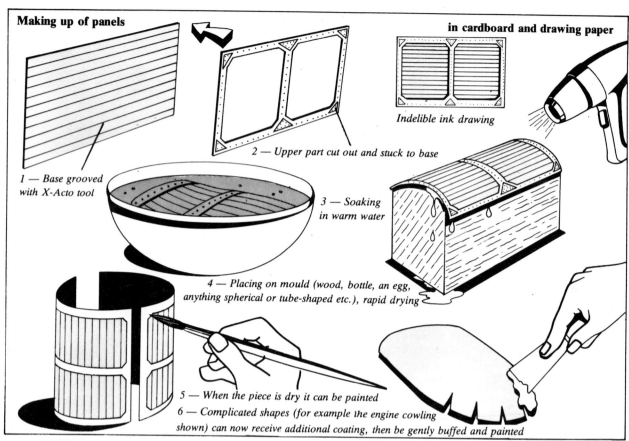

Making up of panels

in cardboard and drawing paper

Indelible ink drawing

2 — Upper part cut out and stuck to base

1 — Base grooved with X-Acto tool

3 — Soaking in warm water

4 — Placing on mould (wood, bottle, an egg, anything spherical or tube-shaped etc.), rapid drying

5 — When the piece is dry it can be painted

6 — Complicated shapes (for example the engine cowling shown) can now receive additional coating, then be gently buffed and painted

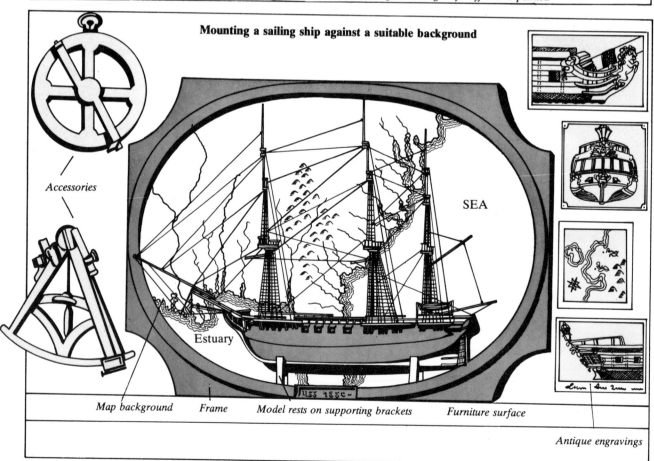

Mounting a sailing ship against a suitable background

Accessories

SEA

Estuary

Map background   *Frame*   *Model rests on supporting brackets*   *Furniture surface*

Antique engravings

Painting on Drawing Paper

Make the basic tracing with a hard-leaded (H) pencil and ruler. Then dilute the paint until you get a very light tint that will simply wash the paper. This can be applied either with a brush or with a foam rubber roller. Ensure that it does not curl the paper. Use only a little colour and the right amount of water, mixed in a bowl. Once the paper is dry, go over the pencil tracing again (it is still visible) with your drawing-pen and compass. The lines should be kept as narrow as possible. Relief and shading effects can be achieved by additional application of water-colour, two or three times stronger than the original tint, using brushes 0 or 1. You can also prepare various water-colours for drawing in details with your pen. If you do this you will have to open the tip a bit wider. The paint must also be carefully mixed: not too runny, and not too thick. The mixture is right if you touch the pen to the end of your finger and it leaves a drop no wider than the nib itself.

Certain special effects are obtained by 'strengthening' the colour. Pencil lead rubbed on with your finger brings out the grain of the paper, which can be made to look like awning, a wall, or material. A similar effect can be achieved by using chalk of exactly the same shade as the paint. Sawdust or sand can be added to the paint to give it a granulated texture (like a wall, for example).

Assembling Drawing Paper and Cardboard

Any model made of drawing paper must be painted first, flat, before the paper is cut. Cutting is easily done, but with a cutter rather than scissors, which never cut perfectly. Drawing paper adheres extremely well to other materials. Because it is so thin it looks real, enhancing the model itself. Shutters, metal surfaces, planking, steps—all can be attached to plastic models by means of liquid glue.

As soon as you use pieces larger than 5cm by 10cm, you must have a backing support. This is often a balsa-wood framework with struts. The best-known backing for a flat surface follows the sketches on page 34 using rectangular or square struts as shown.

Vinyl or other liquid glue may be used

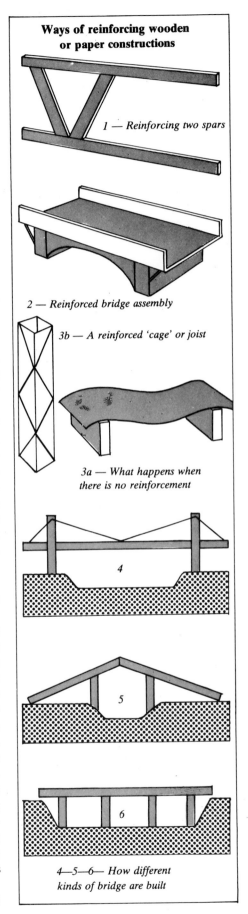

Ways of reinforcing wooden or paper constructions

1 — Reinforcing two spars

2 — Reinforced bridge assembly

3b — A reinforced 'cage' or joist

3a — What happens when there is no reinforcement

4—5—6— How different kinds of bridge are built

for sticking wood and paper. A framework can be reinforced with small modelling pins, which do the same job as the glue.

MODELS MADE OUT OF DRAWING PAPER MUST ALWAYS BE REINFORCED!

Assembling Different Materials (Polystyrene, Wood and Paper)

See the table for the uses of each of these materials in tableaux, models, and dioramas. This is only a rough guide. In following chapters we shall discuss the ideal uses for each of them.

Use and Choice of Materials Depending on Scale				
See glossary for technical characteristics of substances not given as basic modelling materials				
MATERIAL USED	USED FOR	SCALES	PAINT FINISH	ASSEMBLY/CONSTRUCTION
heavy (223g/m²) drawing paper	metal, tiles, planking	1/100−1/25	water-colours, chalk, pencil, china ink	can be joined to polystyrene
thin card	metal, tiles, planking	1/100−1/25	satin-finish, lacquer may be used	can be joined to polystyrene
plastic sections	beams, rafters, metal structures	1/100−1/25	lacquer or acrylic matt paint	compatible with paper, polystyrene and balsa; assembly by glueing
polystyrene sheets	metal, cast-iron, walls, roofs, facades, coachwork	1/72−1/8	lacquer or lacquer-finish paint, intaglio possible	may be stuck edgewise if reinforced; compatible with wood, cardboard, and all modelling materials
thin wood sheeting (poplar, mahogany, etc.)	flying models, boats, ships' decks, painted or varnished wood facades	1/100−1/8	varnish, stain, matt paint (vinyl, acrylic water colours)	vinyl or liquid glue; wood reinforcement; compatible for assembly with paper, cardboard, card
corrugated cardboard (small size, used for packaging)	corrugated iron roofs, corrugated tiling	1/43−1/8	matt paint, water-colours	glueing; assembly compatible with wood, cardboard, paper
cartridge paper	wood-like appearance, may be painted to resemble material	all	water-colours	glueing
Rhodoid	windowpanes, cockpits, water	all	none	glueing; fixing in grooves

coloured Rhodoid	glass roofs, modern glass buildings	all	none	glueing; fixing in grooves
sheets of expanded polystyrene	stonework, rocks, snow, basic scenery	from 1/35	plain, water-colours or acrylics	glueing with special adhesive; sensitive to solvents; compatible for assembly with wood, cardboard, cloth
sawdust	grainy effect for walls and ground	all	all matt paints	in flocking or vinyl glue; mixes in with the paint
granulated cork	ballast, gravel, rock, iron ore	1/100−1/25	plain, water-colours or acrylics	sprinkled or glued directly onto vinyl glue
cork sheeting	walls, roads, other constructions	1/72−1/12	plain	glueing; compatible for assembly with paper, cardboard, wood
metal tubes, rods and sections	all high-fidelity machine components, structures	1/100−1/8	plain or varnished (do not paint, to preserve the metal look)	can be soldered, brazed or clamped; compatible for assembly with wood, polystyrene and plaster
cellulose paste	stonework, countryside	1/100−1/8	paint and flocking	spread with spatula onto fibrous backing
plastic wood	woodwork, filling to look like wood	1/100−1/8	paint or stain	spread with spatula, or plugged
plastic metal	agglomerate that looks like metal	1/8 and up	plain	spread with spatula; shaped with modelling tools
tracing paper	windowpanes television or cinema screens	all	none	glued onto polystyrene, wood, or paper
light ($125g/m^2$) drawing paper	metal, tiles, planking	1/100−1/43	water-colours, chalk, pencil, china ink	glue flat-mounting

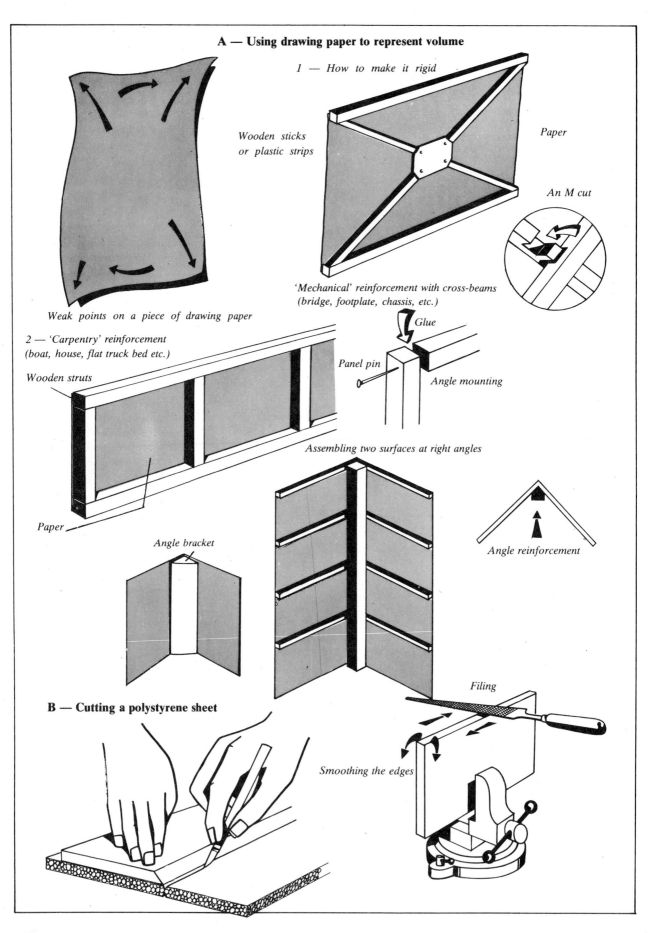

A — Using drawing paper to represent volume

1 — How to make it rigid

Wooden sticks or plastic strips

Paper

An M cut

Weak points on a piece of drawing paper

'Mechanical' reinforcement with cross-beams (bridge, footplate, chassis, etc.)

2 — 'Carpentry' reinforcement (boat, house, flat truck bed etc.)

Wooden struts

Glue

Panel pin

Angle mounting

Paper

Assembling two surfaces at right angles

Angle bracket

Angle reinforcement

B — Cutting a polystyrene sheet

Filing

Smoothing the edges

Plastic Models

In just a few years, these have carved out the lion's share of the market. People, houses, trains, aeroplanes—plastic is everywhere. From 1/100 to 1/8, most models are made out of hard polystyrene plastic. Even 'lead' soldiers are usually plastic today! Now that plastic has become respectable, we must give it pride of place. For the field of plastic models involves all questions of scenery, decoration and finishing touches of all kinds—because if it can be done in plastic, it can be done in other materials. However, let us make one thing clear: like other materials, plastic is not an end in itself. Making a model always involves a careful choice of different materials. Even if it is 90 per cent plastic, the other 10 per cent of plaster, metal, wood or cardboard must be treated with just as much respect. When it comes to modelling in wood or metal, we will confine ourselves to specific instances of their use.

Choosing One's Models

Once you are bitten by the collecting bug, you won't stop at just one particular kind of model. There is always the initial attraction of the kind of thing you like—say motorbikes, or cars, but then you become interested in details, or the historical aspect. But we have no intention of drawing up a catalogue of all the thousands of models available in the shops.

Weapons
Reproduction of weapons on a scale of 1/1 or smaller is comparatively rare. Not many shopkeepers stock such models, and by far the most common among those that do exist are pistols, especially of the Wild West. Once assembled, they are generally used for decorative purposes. They are often mounted as trophies on walls, or framed. Of course they should not be handled too much, and certainly not by inexpert hands. Building up a model gun collection presents no problems, even in a relatively small flat or apartment.

Boats
Plastic ships are not common. Scales range from 1/700 to 1/72 (for landing craft). Historical ships figure largely in all sizes. There are some manufacturers (Heller, Monogram, Tamyia, Revell) who make fleets. A ship collection quickly becomes cumbersome. They are always longer than they are wider and need long shelves for display (or, better, glass cases to avoid dust). Ships with complicated rigging can

Naval models have always been very popular. This is a World War Two German vessel of the same class as the 'Gneisenau' and the 'Scharnhorst'. This is a 1/400 Heller model, and is only 58cm long.

be a problem for the beginner. A classic like the *Royal Sun* needs hours of patience and could never be part of a collection: it must stand alone, with a protective glass case. Using only your spare time, it would take a year to make it!

Utility Machines
These include trucks, tractors and plant machinery. There are not many available and they are usually in scales ranging from 1/43 to 1/20. The most handsome are American (ERTL, AMT), but there are not enough different models to justify making a collection, but a number of them would be suitable for using in large-scale tableaux and dioramas. With only small modifications, foreign models can be made to look like the homegrown variety.

Vintage Cars
The current wave of what is called nostalgia has resulted in an upswing of interest in vintage cars. The first imported models were of 1955–6 American cars. Then came Monogram and Johan models of 1925–39 cars. Unfortunately imports were not sufficiently regular, or were badly followed up. Model cars in general suffered an eclipse between 1970 and 1975. Now, new products and the better continuation of lines means that it is once again possible to collect and build models of vintage cars. The scales are fairly uniform, so you can make genuine collections of famous cars. Numbers can be a problem, but cars can always be displayed on shelves or in a case and, of course, cars can be displayed side-by-side, as in a car park.

One of those odd motor-tricycles which flourished in Britain just before the war.

Motorbikes and Sports Cars

Here again, the choice is expanding. Not only are there the medium-scale racing bikes put out by Protar: there are also wide ranges on larger-scales marketed by Tamyia and Heller. Modern machines are particularly well represented. Sports cars require a certain competence in assembling the mechanical parts, because these remain visible. This also holds good for motorbikes, because the whole point lies in the accurate assembly of parts that will always be seen—chains, engine components, mudguards etc.

Aeroplanes

Model aeroplanes in plastic are numerous. Vintage or contemporary, the widest choice is in the 1939−45 period. Modern planes are well represented too. Planes of the 1960s are also available in large quantities (made by Monogram, Revell, Airfix and Tamyia). Models like these are good for collections, or for use in tableaux that include people, vehicles, equipment and aeroplanes.

Military and Armoured Vehicles

These started to become popular about ten years ago. They are usually in 1/25 or 1/35 and, occasionally, in 1/16. Just about anything that was ever built between 1938 and 1950 is now available in scale-model. You can collect them either 'factory-fresh', or as they are after use and action. Whichever you choose, you can make a

handsome collection in a small flat. Tableaux and dioramas are often too cumbersome.

Most model-makers have something of the historian in them. Behind the pleasure of construction there lies the joy of research into military and civilian machines that were only short-lived. The Potez 540, a French bomber first made in 1930, was out of date by 1939.

Plastic scale-models can help one to become better acquainted with the innumerable tanks made during the 1939–45 war. This Soviet Army Howitzer is one of the many sold by various manufacturers. These models are variations on the K.V.1 gun platforms designed by the Soviet engineer Voroshilov. Regrettably, since 1970, there has been massive duplication in models of tanks from all over the world.

Figures

You can buy soldiers, horses and guns in kits. So not only can you collect people, you can also create scenes where these people are doing things. In general it is very fine work needing great care, especially with regard to colouring. Various companies make troops from 1939 to the present-day—notably Heller, ERTL and Tamyia.

Everyone has his own Speciality

We have seen the various articles that there are for sale, and it seems that each category has its devotees, but since the products available and what can be done

with them have a good deal in common, we will restrict ourselves to studying in detail only the larger categories. Thus scale-models of antique weapons have points in common with any other kind of model, even with motorbikes and sports cars. Technically speaking, models can be categorized in this way:

—figures of historical people;
—vehicles, historical and contemporary;
—military vehicles;
—civilian and military aeroplanes;
—ships, historical and contemporary.

When it comes to tableaux, we shall see further on how each of these categories can fit in with each of the others.

Building the Models

General Principles

Plastic models are sold in assembly kits. A kit contains between 70 and 1,000 or 1,500 moulded components attached to a support called a grid. Each part detaches from the grid and has a reference number. Most manufacturers give each grid a letter (A, B, C, D etc.). So each component has two references: the grid, and its own number (e.g. A1, D29). There are also step-by-step diagrams. The plastic used for the grids is not always the same colour. Each grid will be suitably coloured so that the model-maker who does not wish to paint his model can still assemble it without difficulty, but we do not recommend this procedure: the result is simply a toy, not a real model!

Painting on the Undercoat

Even if the instructions are given in a foreign language (as they sometimes are), the pictures alone usually suffice to show you how to construct the model. It is important to consult the instructions thoroughly, to see where each component goes. Then you can start to paint them.

On being taken out of their bag, parts should be wiped clean. One grid at a time should be placed in a painting container (a milk or fruit juice carton will do very well). Undercoat is applied to the plastic with an aerosol spray, if possible the same colour as the final coat. This is not always easy with military vehicles. Sometimes aerosols are impractical and you must use a brush. Select the largest one practicable for the parts, so that the paint will be as even as possible. The undercoat will diminish the semi-shiny look of the natural plastic, making it either matt or glossy, depending on the model being made.

Always apply paint with successive light strokes, as when using a paint-gun. Do not hold the can too close.

Cutting off and Preparing the Parts

The parts should not be detached or prepared before they are needed for assembly. It is also a good idea not to handle them directly, but only with tweezers or fine pliers. (Drying-time, anything from a few minutes to several hours, must elapse between application of undercoat and detachment from the grid). Once it is detached, each part will have a little bump at the point where it was attached. This must be removed with a fine-grained file (a nail file, for example). Make sure that all parts are correctly smoothed in this manner before glueing. Any excess paint remaining from the previous stage may also have to be removed by scraping.

This is how the separate parts look once they have been made. These are the various components of a French Empire field-gun, (made by Historex).

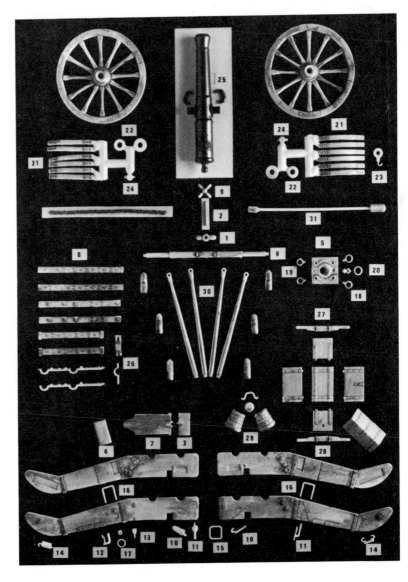

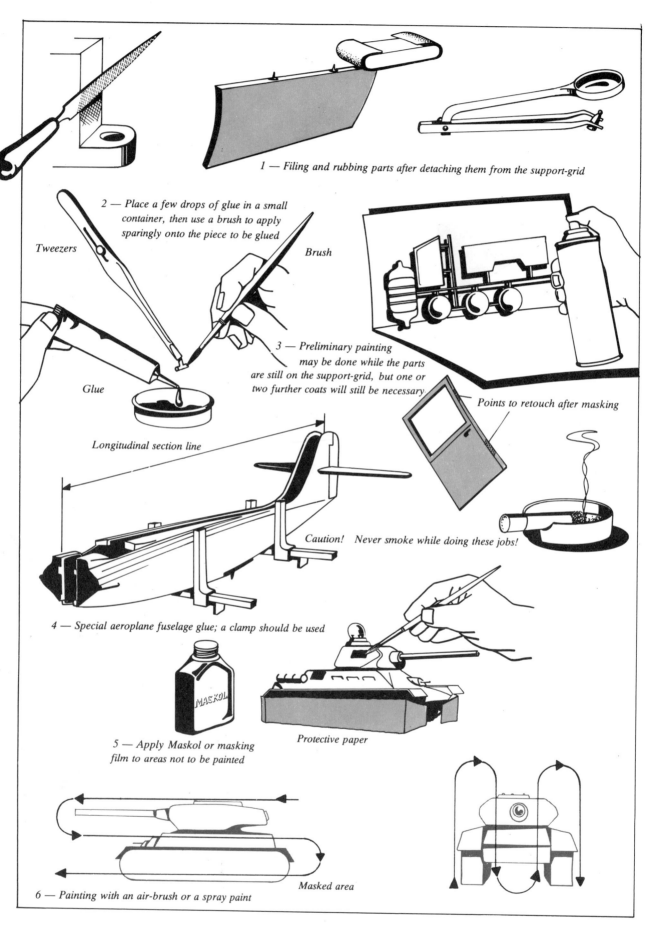

1 — Filing and rubbing parts after detaching them from the support-grid

2 — Place a few drops of glue in a small container, then use a brush to apply sparingly onto the piece to be glued

Tweezers

Brush

Glue

3 — Preliminary painting may be done while the parts are still on the support-grid, but one or two further coats will still be necessary.

Points to retouch after masking

Longitudinal section line

Caution! Never smoke while doing these jobs!

4 — Special aeroplane fuselage glue; a clamp should be used

MASKOL

5 — Apply Maskol or masking film to areas not to be painted

Protective paper

6 — Painting with an air-brush or a spray paint

Masked area

Glueing

Never apply glue directly from the tube or container to components to be assembled. Use only special glue for scale-models. Never use so-called plastic glues. Squeeze a small amount of glue onto a saucer. Take a fine brush, already dipped into the appropriate solvent or thinner, and apply a tiny drop of glue to one of the pieces to be glued. Then take a pair of fine pliers and join the two pieces together. For especially long or cumbersome pieces, a modeller's clamp will ensure that they do not come apart. Remove any excess drops of glue at once with the point of an X-Acto tool. Some people remove excess glue with a thinner, but this does not work for all models. To secure very small pieces, hold one in an X-tra hand tool or an alligator clip and the other in a pair of tweezers.

All these stages, which seem obvious, are often forgotten by modellers and, as a result, their first efforts are often ruined by carelessness in glueing.

Finishing off one Component Part of a Model

Once you have assembled all the pieces of one component part of the model, you must finish it off: remove all traces of glue, make sure assembly is correct, retouch paintwork. A model generally has three or four major component parts. It's up to you to decide whether certain details should be finished off now or at the end. Your procedure may vary from one model to another. Ageing of parts, for example (to make a machine or a tank or a house look used or dirty), can be done very quickly. (See the section on painting for how to do it).

Sticking on Transfers

Nearly every model, of no matter what, comes with transfers. They can be applied now, or at the end. It is not difficult to do. The transfer is on a cellulose backing that comes off when you place it in water, so cut out the transfer and put it in a saucer or glass of water. Smear a light coating of water (just a few drops) with your finger on the exact place on the model where the transfer will be applied. Then, when the transfer has come away from its backing, lift it out with two pairs of tweezers to stop

it rolling up. Apply it as accurately as you can to the wet spot on the model. Holding it in place with one pair of tweezers in the left hand, you then remove excess water with a piece of absorbent cotton in the right hand. Finally, press the transfer into place with a piece of blotting paper.

Assembly

Major components of models are usually held together with glue. We do not recommend the use of elastic bands to hold pieces together while the glue is drying. It is better always to use special model

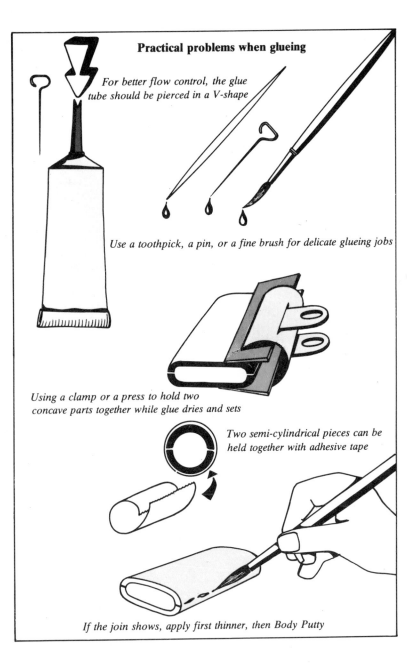

Practical problems when glueing

For better flow control, the glue tube should be pierced in a V-shape

Use a toothpick, a pin, or a fine brush for delicate glueing jobs

Using a clamp or a press to hold two concave parts together while glue dries and sets

Two semi-cylindrical pieces can be held together with adhesive tape

If the join shows, apply first thinner, then Body Putty

clamps. To ensure that larger components, such as aeroplane fuselages, decks of ships or bases of buildings stick efficiently, it is sometimes necessary to give them a light roughening with a file or other abrasive. Too much glue never improves anything! Once assembly is complete, there are various kinds of masking papers or tapes which can be applied to those parts that will not be painted. A product like Maskol will do this job very well. It should be applied with a brush, and allowed to dry for fifteen minutes. You may then proceed with the finishing stages.

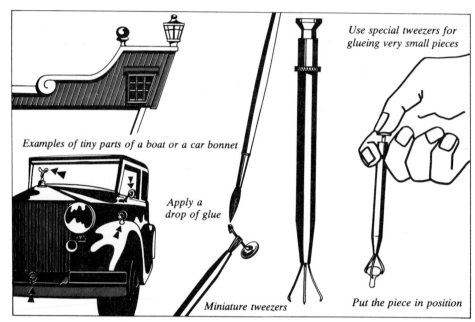

Examples of tiny parts of a boat or a car bonnet

Apply a drop of glue

Use special tweezers for glueing very small pieces

Miniature tweezers

Put the piece in position

Tips for painting

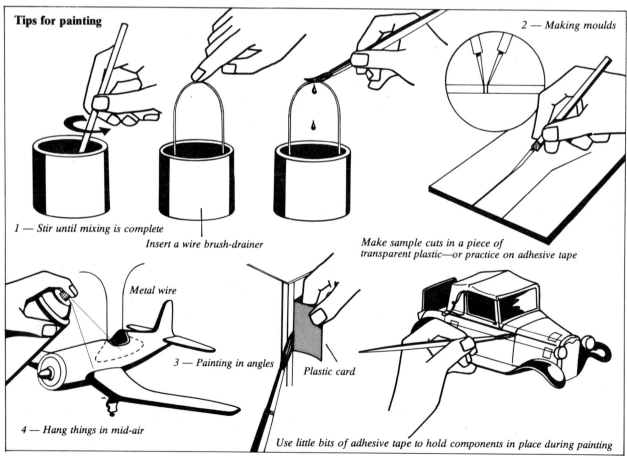

1 — Stir until mixing is complete

Insert a wire brush-drainer

2 — Making moulds

Make sample cuts in a piece of transparent plastic—or practice on adhesive tape

Metal wire

3 — Painting in angles

Plastic card

4 — Hang things in mid-air

Use little bits of adhesive tape to hold components in place during painting

Finishing

We will deal in a later chapter with the overall setting of a model, lighting and scenery etc. For the moment we are concerned with the finishing details. A coat of air-brush paint, well thinned and therefore all the more matt, can be made to look like dust, rust or soot. A few details applied with a '0' or a '00' brush will supply the perfect finish. A road-map, or a suitcase ready beside a car, gives the appearance of a journey about to start; soldiers round an armoured vehicle make the scene a briefing; barrels beside a boat are another touch of reality. You must use your imagination. Remember: before you put a model in place in a tableau, you must submit it to 'weathering', so that it matches the environment and the supposed climatic conditions, but for display in a glass case, weathering is not always desirable.

We make no mention here of certain details which the experts never omit in their models. This usually involves the

addition of minute details: wiring and pipes on vehicles, medals and epaulettes on soldiers, and so on. We will look at particular examples when we come to technique.

Above: Detail of a German Leopard A2 tank gun-turret after 'weathering'. 1/35 model made from a Heller kit.

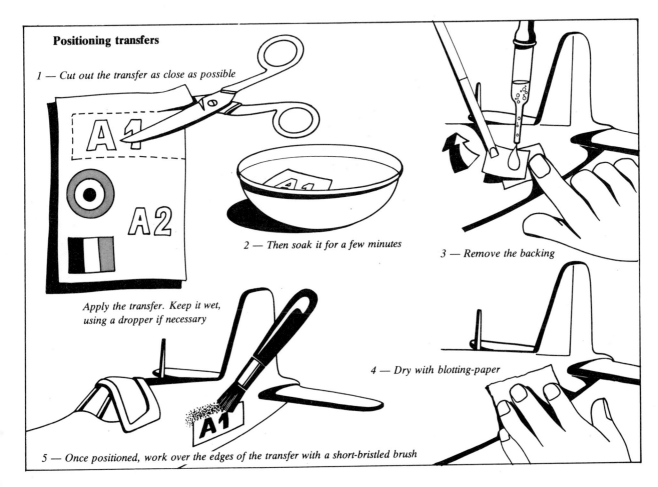

Positioning transfers

1 — Cut out the transfer as close as possible

2 — Then soak it for a few minutes

3 — Remove the backing

Apply the transfer. Keep it wet, using a dropper if necessary

4 — Dry with blotting-paper

5 — Once positioned, work over the edges of the transfer with a short-bristled brush

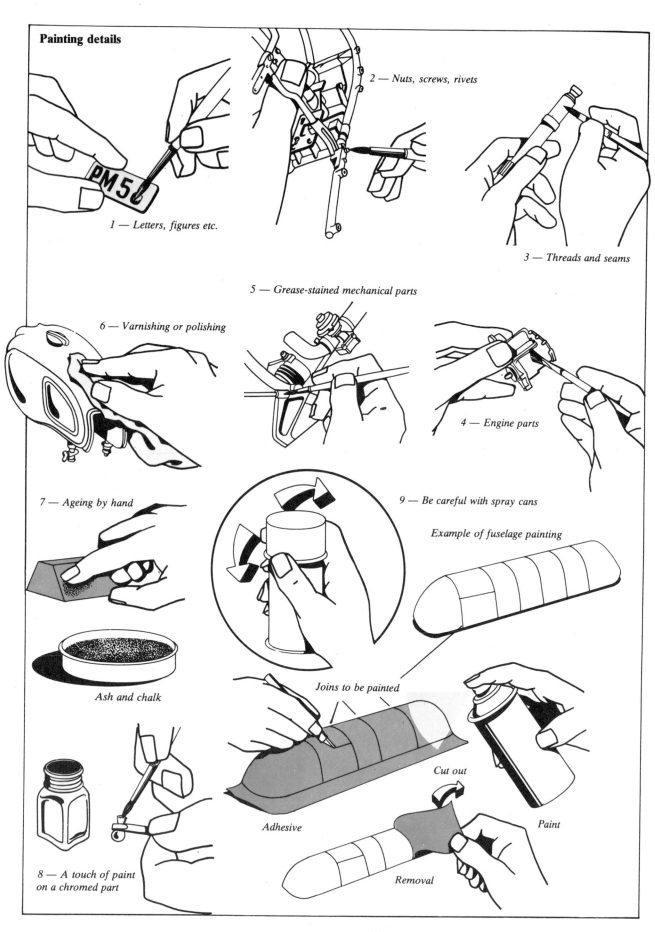

Painting details

1 — Letters, figures etc.

2 — Nuts, screws, rivets

3 — Threads and seams

5 — Grease-stained mechanical parts

6 — Varnishing or polishing

4 — Engine parts

7 — Ageing by hand

9 — Be careful with spray cans

Example of fuselage painting

Ash and chalk

Joins to be painted

Cut out

8 — A touch of paint on a chromed part

Adhesive

Removal

Paint

For Further Information

There are clubs and associations where people interested in every kind of model making can meet each other. Also, for information, there are a number of British and American publications, e.g. 'Scale Modeller', 'Military Modelling', and 'Scale-Models'. In every country there is an information and contact office of the IPMS (International Plastic Model Society).

Taking a look at what is available in the shops, we have to admit that there are gaps in plastic model ranges, with the result that by no means will every customer be satisfied. There are almost no quality models at all on the Middle Ages or the Roman era. The saga of the Far West does equally badly, with only a few railroad models available. In the 1/72, the 1/35, and the 1/25 ranges, there are also various accessories missing: street furnishings in particular, and others.

List of International Plastic Model correspondents (Europe, Canada)

IPMS — Great Britain:
J.W. Salmon, 'Oakbank', 35 Clares Green Road, Spencers Wood, Reading, RG7 1DY.
Publication: *IPMS Magazine* (every two months)

IPMS — Belgium:
Guy Gudenkauf, Ancien Dieweg 9, 1180 Brussels
Publication: *Kit* (quarterly)

IPMS — Canada:
E.A. Johnson, IPMS Canada, P.O. Box 626, Ottawa (Stn B), Ontario.
Publication: *R.T.* (monthly)

IPMS — Denmark:
Willy Larsen, Buskager 20, II, DK-2720 Vanlose.
Publication: *Halehjulet*

IPMS — France:
Saint-Ouen l'Aumône 95310.
Publication: *La Vitrine du Maquettiste*

IPMS — Germany:
Gunther Lindow, Bauingenieur, 1000 Berlin 37, Oertzenweg 12b.
Publication: *Mitteljungen* (monthly)

IPMS — Holland:
H.C. Beentjes, Naarden, 1352 Van Houtenlaan 10.
Publication: *Modelbouw in Plastic* (quarterly)

IPMS — Italy:
A.M. Bellei, Via U. Balzani 8, 00162 Rome, I.
Publication: *Il Notiziario* (quarterly)

IPMS — Norway:
Tom Arheim, Asperudeien II, Oslo 12.
Publication: *Limtuben*

IPMS — Sweden:
Hans Percy, Onskevadersgaten 47, S-417 35 Goteborg.

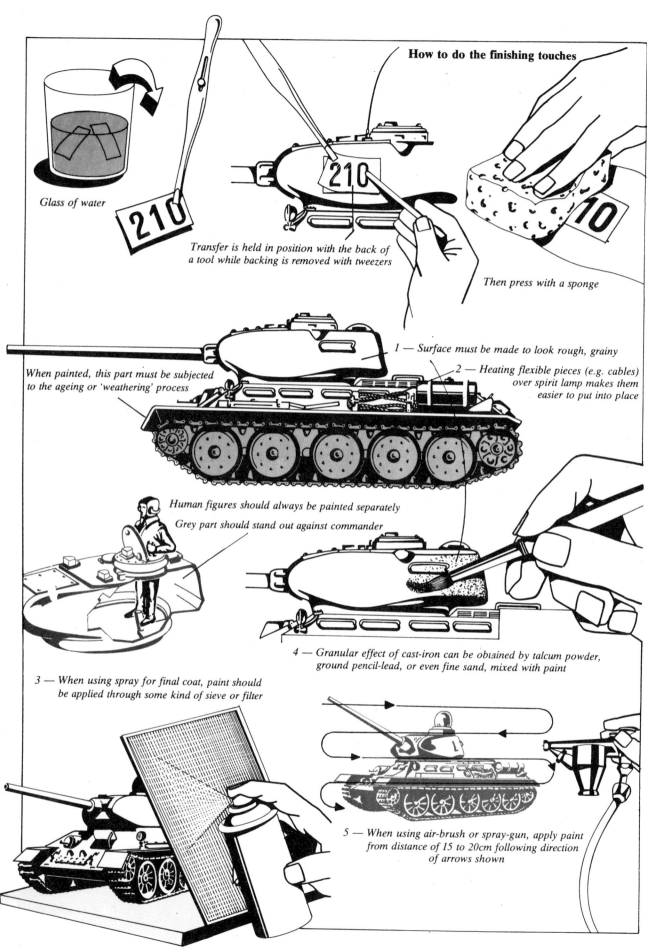

How to do the finishing touches

Glass of water

Transfer is held in position with the back of
a tool while backing is removed with tweezers

Then press with a sponge

When painted, this part must be subjected
to the ageing or 'weathering' process

1 — Surface must be made to look rough, grainy

2 — Heating flexible pieces (e.g. cables)
over spirit lamp makes them
easier to put into place

Human figures should always be painted separately

Grey part should stand out against commander

4 — Granular effect of cast-iron can be obtained by talcum powder,
ground pencil-lead, or even fine sand, mixed with paint

3 — When using spray for final coat, paint should
be applied through some kind of sieve or filter

5 — When using air-brush or spray-gun, apply paint
from distance of 15 to 20cm following direction
of arrows shown

Your Models: The Finishing Touches

Having read this far, the beginner knows enough to avoid major mistakes, but he must now acquire the necessary practical experience, for which there is no substitute. This know-how should be accompanied by various special skills and knowledge of certain particular methods. So this chapter is a sort of list of knacks, of skills that will provide ideas, rather than a course of instruction for the gifted pupil.

Painting

In the preceding chapter, we considered this from the undercoat angle. Let us now see how, with a little dexterity, we can do an even better job. We have discussed the various possibilities of paintwork. To start with, the beginner will use basically the brush and the spray-can. Then, raising his standards, and seeing the models of his friends and relations, he wants the paintwork on his own to be rather better, so he finds out about the air-brush.

How do you use an Air-Brush?

It is used to vaporize cellulose paints, matt paints, thinner, water-colours etc. You hold it like a pencil, the index finger resting on the air flow control. The paint is carried in a glass container underneath. The amount of air released is controlled by means of a knurled wheel. Propulsion is provided by a liquid-gas container. With the air-brush in position 'A', the flow is powerful, concentrated and fine. In position 'B' it is wider and more gentle. One of the major advantages of the air-brush is that successive coats of paint can be applied without underlying details becoming blurred. It is the ideal tool for doing skies, dust, camouflage, and for such things as a horse's dappled coat. The air-brush highlights irregularities in any surface, which often enhances the effect of volume. With lined or grooved balsa-wood, the air-brush immediately gives a relief effect, but it also highlights mistakes!

As with painting by brush, the preparation of the paint itself is of prime importance. Thinner and paint should be mixed until a fluid, creamy texture is obtained. If it is too creamy, the painted surface will have an 'orange-skin' look. It it is too fluid, it will drip. Make a few tests before painting the actual model. You must also remember that the more thinner used, the more matt the paint will be. For a correct matt mixture, use one part of thinner to two parts of paint. For the first coat, use the concentrated paint-flow and paint from right to left and then from top to bottom—always holding the air-brush at the same distance from the model. After drying (at least half a day), the final coat may be applied, very thinly. Two undercoats are usually needed, and then either one or two final coats. With small areas, it is often necessary to apply sticky paper or masking tape to the surfaces that should not be painted. This will sharply delineate the painted area.

Preparation of Surfaces

Care in preparing surfaces is just as important as knowing how to use the air-brush. Metal surfaces must be cleaned with trichloroethylene. Plastics must be thoroughly dust-free, and should often be washed in warm soapy water.

After Use

A badly cleaned air-brush may be unusable, so any paint remaining after use must be removed. The container must be washed two or three times in thinner. When all visible traces of paint have gone, fill it about one-third full with thinner and operate the air-flow control for a few seconds—until the thinner is coming through colourless. Cotton-wool and cotton-waste should not be used for cleaning, as these leave fibres that will obstruct the holes. To protect the air-brush from dust, place an empty paint container upside-down over it.

The Technical Possibilities of the Air-Brush

As we shall see below, with aeroplanes and military vehicles, the air-brush permits all kinds of colouring, particularly the merging of colours with each other. In general, experience shows that the

Flak (anti-aircraft) gun, remark-
able for its finer details. Made
from a Tamyia kit, this model
has a number of personal
touches—ammunition-box,
camouflage netting.

application of matt paint is easier than gloss, which tends to run. Drying time can often be six hours or more. Drying *must* be done in a dust-free environment and at normal room temperature. Do not use a hair-dryer as this may result in wrinkles in the paint. With larger surfaces, such as a ship's hull, coachwork, an aeroplane fuse-lage, the air-brush ensures even applica-tion of paint. With a large surface of this kind, make sure while working that the paint mixture remains consistent and that the glass container stays horizontal.

What about Special Effects or Marks in the Paintwork?

Grease, mud, dust and oil-leaks are all details that one might wish to reproduce on realistic scale-models. For this, the model-maker should have among his equipment a medium brush with the bristles cut off to one-third their length. Using paint with almost no thinner, and allowing it partially to dry in the air, dip the brush into the paint and dab it onto the piece to be painted. In this way you can achieve a very satisfying dirty or ageing effect. If the dab-marks look too pronoun-ced, you can reduce them somewhat by re-applying the undercoat colour in the same manner.

Facing page: These pictures
are so lifelike that they would
scare readers if they appeared in
a magazine.
Top left: A Red Army T34.
Below: A Chevrolet-Canada
used by British troops in Africa.

What about the Finishing Touches on Glass-Case Display Models?

Starting with 'glass' components, such as headlamps, cockpit canopies and windows, cover the whole model with either a satin-effect (non-glossy) or a gloss varnish. This should be done at a temperature of around 20 °C; the air should not be humid, as this might cause the varnish to wrinkle. Ensure too that your varnish will not harm any transfers used. Protective varnish of this kind will tend to hide imperfections in painting without reducing the details. Note that this procedure should not be followed with figures of people, which need a special finish of their own (see chapter on figures).

The Special Case of Military Models

We will deal with the particular problems of armoured vehicles later on. Whether your model is of a tank, a half-track, an army truck or a plane, it is better to apply only one undercoat to individual pieces and larger component parts. The rest of the painting should be done when the whole model is assembled. This will give a rough look, which the real thing would have. Placing transfers on just before the final coat will give them a used look. This final coat, often called a wash, is a mixture of much-thinned paint and solvent. To give a dusty appearance (a vehicle that has been on a long expedition, or for desert battle scenes), special dust (in the Floquil weathering kit) may be applied. This final coat will give a dusty white effect on drying, while remaining quite transparent.

Special Case: Particular Mechanical Parts

Some motorbike and racing car engines, and some aeroplane parts, have complex shapes and should generally be painted in glossy or bright-coloured paint. This may of course tend to block up certain holes. To avoid this problem, it is a good idea to apply first a matt primer; this will provide sufficient surface-tension to prevent the running of the second coat. To help the undercoat behave, first wash the surface with acetone applied with a brush and let it dry. Sometimes just the action of the acetone on the surface of the plastic is enough to allow application of the final coat. Some modellers prefer to polish after application of the undercoat—although this may not always be possible (with engine-housing, for example).

Facing page: A very effective setting for reconnaissance vehicles made from Tamyia kits. Below: Very fine model of a British artillery piece. All these models are excellent examples of quality finishing.

The art of adding the finishing touches. On both these 1/35 1939–45 tanks, the model-maker has done everything possible to make them look authentic: dull grainy paintwork, marks of use, and browning of the metal make these look like photographs of the real thing.

49

American produced civilian models are still not widely known. In the States there is a certain predilection for heavy-duty trucks. This White 1/25 model of a semi-articulated lorry has about 250 separate parts to assemble.

Making Plastic look like Metal

The metal frameworks and other components of big guns, machine guns and rifles are most often black. On real metal, this colouring is due to the phosphating of steel. With a scale-model, you can do as follows: paint the barrel and the breech black. When dry, lightly wash with a very light grey wash and immediately wipe it off. The lighter colour will remain only on projections—rivets, screws, pins etc. Next, scrape a little soft pencil-lead into a jar. Dip a dry brush into the powder that results, and cover the entire body or framework of the weapon with it. This will give it a very realistic metal look. This technique can also be used for stairways and ships' rails, as well as various bits of machinery. For copper components, simply substitute gold-dust (a painting colour!) for the pencil-lead, and a very light-green wash for the grey wash. If a metal part needs to look used but not rusty, prepare the following mixture: two-parts of cigarette ash to one-part of soft pencil-lead (2B), applied to the part after painting. Or, for the oxidized look of exhaust pipes and springs that are exposed to the elements, make a powder from yellow and ochre drawing chalks. Vary the proportions to obtain the desired hue, then

apply as before, after painting with thinned ochre-beige. In order to make screws and rivets stand out, or all metal parts that are subject to friction (e.g. pulley-grooves, handrails, cables, plough-shares, ships' screws), the procedure is slightly different. The part is painted black or matt grey, and then given a coating of silver diluted with turpentine. Then with the finger apply some picture framer's 'silver' powder. This will give a polished-metal effect similar to the effects of friction. (The powder is available as Rub 'n' Buff).

Making Plastic look like Wood

Pieces of balsa-wood will never look like real wood. The impressions of both weight and colour must be created. Ships' decks, truck sides and shop fronts are all made to look like wood in the same way. An appropriate undercoat is applied:

—grey-green for wood susceptible to mould or mildew;
—silvery-grey for wood that has aged and remained dry;
—light brown for painted wood.

After the undercoat is dry, with a pencil trace the grain and knots in the wood, then make some stand out with fine paintbrush work in the same colour. After drying,

A modern heavy-duty vehicle from the United States. These spectacular and colourful models have a number of chromed parts for extra effect. The principal American manufacturers of such models are Mack, H1 (International), and White.

apply a matt ageing wash. Finish by rubbing with chalk or pencil-lead powder (brown, black or grey). A burnt-wood effect is easily obtained by rubbing the component with genuine charcoal.

Final Glueing

Earlier on we gave you the simplest methods of glueing, but rubbing down and sticking together do not always suffice. To begin with, moulded parts are seldom joined along the same lines as their real-life counterparts—hulls of ships, for example, or the join between shoulder and arm on a figure.

So after glueing (forty-five minutes to one hour), in accordance with the previous chapter, apply a reasonably fluid substance called Body Putty over the entire joint, with a spatula or the end of the finger. Allow to dry for an hour, then rub with a soft abrasive dipped in water. Rub until the line of the join is no longer visible and can no longer be felt. Take this opportunity also to remove finally all excess glue. The tip of an X-Acto tool is good for this.

Use Solvents Correctly

Different solvents—nail polish remover (amyl acetate), acetone and trichloroethylene—have different effects on different kinds of plastic. They can be used to clean paint brushes, to thin paint, or to etch plastic. We strongly advise the beginner to experiment with each kind of plastic and paint.

The professional and expert model-makers consulted on this subject have differing opinions. Some have abandoned tubes of glue in favour of bottles of powerful solvent which they apply to pieces to be assembled. A brush dipped in solvent is applied to the surfaces to be glued, and then simple pressure serves to 'solder' them together. There is invariably an interaction between solvent and plastic. A smooth, satiny surface can be roughened by brushing with a solvent. Take care that before using thinner or any of the standard commercial solvents, transparent plastic parts are thoroughly protected. Solvent will make them irreversibly opaque. Sometimes this effect can be actively sought—for instance, to give the effect of rain and mud on windscreens.

Solvents generally make paints runnier—but sometimes they make them lumpy, or produce a wrinkled or crackled effect. Here again, it is useful to experiment first.

Finally, a use people often do not think of: cleaning the fingers! But beware—most solvents are harmful to the skin and they are all inflammable!

Useful Tricks for an even Better Finish

Scale, and Detail of Paintwork

All the component parts of your model are now painted. They need only a few additional details. Engines of ships, planes etc. need particular attention, to show off oxidized parts or oil stains. We will deal with this problem when we discuss each particular kind of model. As a general rule, a thin coat of turpentine mixed with a drop of black paint and a dash of silver will 'age' metal components. If a building needs to be lit always from the same angle, effects of shade can be heightened by means of turpentine mixed with brown, while the lit side is painted in lighter colours. When it comes to painting windows, glass roofs etc., so that everything except the cross-

Air-brush used to spray 'mud' paint

Two small pieces of adhesive tape

After drying, remove the masks

Then attach two fine strips of plastic to represent the wipers

Making a dirty windscreen

When the model becomes the real thing! This wagon, made by Historex, is not much bigger than a box of matches. Despite this, note the delicacy of the moulding and the quality of the paintwork—even more extraordinary when you realise that the model is smaller than the photograph.

pieces looks transparent, the latter should be protected with adhesive tape. The tape should be cut accurately and the paint applied evenly.

Just as it is amusing to see the eyes and lips of a scale-model human figure, so there are certain details on particular aircraft that are worth bringing out in relief. On the other hand, with a diorama these details should be hidden so as not to detract from the general effect. At 1/35 or 1/72, one would not bother with an aeroplane rivet the size of a coin, or with the iris and pupil in the eye of a human figure! This would be excessive technique, not commensurate with the scale. It should be remembered too that a soldier in battle has a contorted, puckered face, the skin grey rather than pink.

Moving Parts: Finishing Touches to Machinery

A few moments' thought are needed when it comes to the making of the wheels of a vehicle, a field-gun being towed along, a sail being hoisted, or a smoking chimney. Tyres, for example, should be slightly flattened once fitted, to give the impression of weight bearing down on them. It is best in most cases to paint the tyres a neutral matt shade, even if the real thing is black, to escape the rather unrealistic plastic look.

Here is the way to put a tread on your tyres. Take a fine-grained file (choose one that will match the scale of the model), and heat it up in near-boiling water. Roll the

tyre quickly along the file. Since it is hot, it will leave its own impression on the plastic.

This is how to model the effects of smoke, or exhaust fumes. Set light to a piece of polystyrene (open the window first) over a candle. You can use the thick smoke that it gives off to dirty up a model or a component, just like an engine that has been running long hours (a tank, a boat, a car etc.).

Wires and Cables: Basic Technique

Of course there are various methods for various models, depending on scale, but here is a simple way of making radio antennae or ropes, when stringing nylon threads from point to point will not do. Take the model's support-grid, and select one of the little connecting stubs (not too big). Hold this over a flame and pull. When it gets soft and strung out, quickly

Lights are merciless on scale-models. These (Heller) French infantrymen of 1939–45 are delicately and realistically painted: nothing is over-shiny, and their uniforms look realistically coarse.

A model is well finished and truly complete if the parts you cannot see are as well worked on and assembled as those you can. All the details of the 8-cylinder overhead camshaft engine have been reproduced on this 1930s Alfa Romeo two-seater. Plug leads and speedometer cables are all there.

bend it into the required shape. The plastic will cool almost immediately and will keep its shape. Using a pair of electric pliers, cut it to the desired length.

Problems with Models which the Enthusiast must know about

We have kept this section until now, so as not to put you off—and to enable you to correct imperfections in the light of what you have already learned. The publishers of some magazines spend quite a lot of time compiling lists of mistakes and inaccuracies in the models you can buy for

assembly. Some mistakes only worry the purist, while others are more glaring. Furthermore, relief work is often enhanced by 'forcing' details a little, especially on 1/72 and 1/83 models, rivets, handles and plugs are often made absolutely huge.

Cheaper models in particular tend to have the worst faults at present. There are certain aspects of assembly which seem easy enough to the manufacturer, but which only work one time in three for the purchaser. Examples of these are tracks on tanks, working steering wheels on lorries and cars, and the electric motors of self-

Everything we have just said about vintage models (previous page) is true of modern vehicles. Tip the cab on this semi-articulated lorry, and the machinery is all there, just like the real thing. Note especially the corrugated non-slip foot-plates. The beginner must be particularly careful with any moving parts like doors and bonnets, which may not always work perfectly.

powered electric models. Doors, hatches and lockers should all open properly—but you must check the quality of the hinges if you want them to work. Of course, the manufacturer does not tell you this! There are a number of quality models that are meant for model-makers well versed in assembly; they are not recommended for beginners—apart from anything else, the parts are not marked for identification.

Inaccuracy in a model can be partly rectified by research in specialist books and magazines. Sometimes it is a good idea to make sketches on paper to see how the model could be improved if, for example, it were lengthened or shortened.

Odds and Ends

Where to keep them?

Before going on to deal with each kind of scale-model, let us suggest that you obtain a large box or a set of containers for keeping various odds and ends for future use: .22 cartridge casings, paper-clips, pins, thread, pebbles, broken toys etc. Modelling calls for things of all shapes, cylindrical, cubic and flat. Certain everyday things like facial tissues, ends of material and matches should be kept carefully. Their uses will be unlimited.

What can be done with them?

Your best adviser is always your own imagination. We shall return in a later chapter to the uses of odds and ends in large tableaux, for things like buildings, fields and scenery. For the moment, let us see how they can improve a model by making it more realistic. With a large-scale model, a china ink bottle can be an acetylene cylinder; a blown-out fuse can be either a lamp standard or a wall bracket, depending on the scale. Disposable paper handkerchiefs present a host of possibilities, from making sails and tent-cloth, to clothes for human figures. With simple sawdust, painted various colours, you can make a realistic green lawn, or a gravel surface (grey, brown). Metal or plastic insect netting has many unsuspected uses—indeed it is almost indispensable to the model-maker. It can be used for gratings, barred windows, landing strips and ships' hatchways. Before being positioned, the metal should be given a coat of matt paint in the desired colour, to dull it. Unwanted veining etc. can be filled over the Body Putty.

Cyanoacrylate glue should be used for such assembly—or, on wood for example, an ordinary plastic glue.

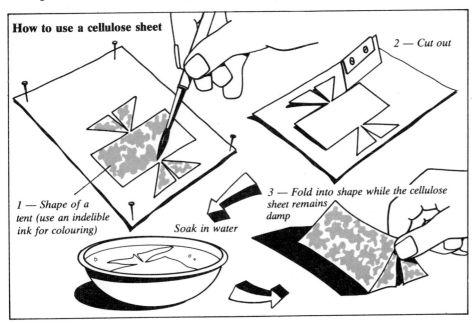

How to use a cellulose sheet

2 — Cut out

1 — Shape of a tent (use an indelible ink for colouring)

Soak in water

3 — Fold into shape while the cellulose sheet remains damp

A personal touch always adds a great deal to a model. Here, two linen threads and a piece of hessian add a realistic note to the rear of this 1940–44 motorcycle and sidecar combination.

Making your own Transfers

Transfers are part of just about every scale-model. There are a huge number available for use on such military items as aeroplanes or tanks. For 'civilian' items, the choice is smaller, even sometimes non-existent: posters, hoardings, directions, road signs. Of course, the transfer you need may not go perfectly with the scale of the model, so here is a way of making your own transfers to stick onto your own models. You should use the plain (unmarked) part of the ordinary transfers you can buy. Choose the shapes, letters, designs etc. that you need in Letraset, and make up your own sign with them, but you will say, why not just apply them directly onto the model? Quite simply, because they easily may not stick properly to plywood, or to plastic, or to a curved surface, but if they are mounted on a regular transfer sheet, the sheet itself will stick to anything.

In the same way you can paint with a '00' brush (using a magnifying glass).

Home-made transfers should be applied slightly moist. Cutting should be done with scissors and *in situ*.

Models of all kinds

Making and Displaying Figures

With very few exceptions, the age of lead soldiers is dead. More and more frequently, the figures in model making are made out of plastic. There are some mediocre models to be had in the small scales (1/43, 1/48 and 1/100) which could do with improvement. The larger scales (1/35, 1/25, 1/12 and 1/8) yield more detailed products, which indeed in some cases are real masterpieces. The Historex company of France, which specializes in making figures of Napoleonic times, offers soldiers to assemble and paint that are extraordinarily accurate. There are various companies (Heller, Tamyia, Historex and Esci) producing satisfactory models of present-day soldiers as well as those of 1939−45.

The modeller who would like to set up scenes that include figures finds himself up against the problem of models made with classic gestures and attitudes—the soldier mounted, famous person seated, the figure making some standard gesture. These are not too difficult to alter and, indeed, it is nearly always necessary.

Working the Material

As with other plastic models, the basic tool is the cutter. You will also need a few chisels, files and jeweller's saws. (See the section on basic tools).

The effects of the solvent trichloroethylene are sometimes hard to predict. However, it can be used to dissolve small pieces of plastic. The viscous liquid that results can itself be used to retouch clothes or even the faces of figures. It can also serve as a cement or a filler. Similar results are obtained by mixing liquid glue with plastic shavings. Body Putty can also be used.

Altering and Improving Models

The wooden tailor's dummy is sometimes recommended for studying positions of the human body, but these days it is a very expensive item. A good substitute is the 'Action Man' type articulated model. The limbs of this figure all move in the same way as real joints. A small notch is cut with either a slitting file or a three-square file.

To change the position of an arm or a leg, hold the notched part over a cold flame (spirit lamp). Obviously this must be done *before any painting is attempted*. If a notch is too wide it can be packed with filler prepared in advance; any lumps caused by stretching can be removed with an X-Acto tool.

Certain parts of a figure, for example the hands, or the feet when there are no boots, benefit from being separated from the rest and re-attached in the final desired position. A pyrograph (see chapter on know-how) is used to obtain positions different from the original. People are generally tempted to add extra details and personal touches to the model they have just bought. There are all kinds of things you can buy to make life-like improvements. Painted crêpe will serve as an individual's camouflage-net, while a back-pack can be made out of small pieces of felt. Gas-masks are made of .22 cartridge cases. Toilet paper or paper towelling soaked in paint and plasticizer can be used for cloaks, capes, or other articles of clothing. Horsehair gathered on a drop of glue, then cut with scissors, can make a horse's mane or the plume on a military hat. A furry appearance can be produced with coloured absorbent cotton.

Boxes of accessories (Heller, Tamyia, Historex) allow you to create a suitable environment for your figures—road-signs, tools and hand guns are available at 1/35, 1/43 and 1/48, for you to add your own personal touch.

Painting a Figure Properly

This is really quite an art, and everyone has his own tricks. For figures, you have a choice between water-colours and acrylic paints. We suggest you do not use oils, as these take too long to dry. Water-colours should be mixed with ox-gall: if not, they will be difficult to apply and will 'bead' on the plastic. Their matt quality gives excellent visual results. As a general rule, and whatever paint you choose, use colours lighter than they are in real life. So black hair should become a mouse-grey shade, bright red epaulettes should be brick-red, and the bright white of a shirt-front or a flag should be off-white. When you reduce something from life-size to a scale of 1/35,

not *all* intensity of colour disappears, but about half does.

Faces and hands are first painted in flesh tone. Then slightly darker shading (1/3 more paint, or a touch of brown) is applied to the sides of the nose, the cheekbones and the eyebrows. All work should be done with a '0' or a '00' brush. Using a plastic scrap for testing, obtain the shade for beard stubble on men's faces by mixing a much diluted grey with the flesh tone. For finishing arms, faces and hands, the best ingredients to work with are flesh tone, white, yellow and brown. They should be diluted in a container with water and applied in a series of little touches to give relief to each detail. For extra-fine shading detail, dip the brush in plain water. Eyes should be drawn with a single brown line shading off towards the eyelids—or painted realistically; but this is necessary only for larger-scale models. First the eyeball is painted in white, and then the iris with a touch of brown, blue or green, using a '00' brush. Some modellers go so far as to put in the pupil with a point of black. To bring out the details of various parts, such as hands, lips and nose, a brick-red wash can be applied lightly; it is then diluted. Details of clothing, folds etc. are obtained by shading all tones into grey—greenish-grey, pure grey, brown, sandy etc. This technique also gives fullness to curtains, awnings and flags. Parts in relief are made somewhat lighter by the addition of a little solvent, while folds and hollows are coloured slightly darker.

French Imperial troops at attention

Positions of horses

Standing still

The trot

The canter

Eating or drinking

The walk

Horse at full gallop

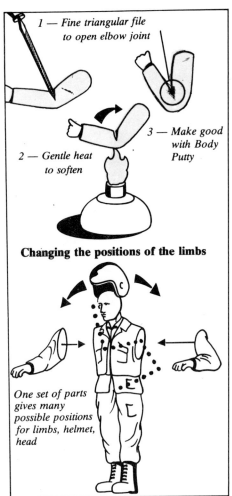

1 — Fine triangular file to open elbow joint

2 — Gentle heat to soften

3 — Make good with Body Putty

Changing the positions of the limbs

One set of parts gives many possible positions for limbs, helmet, head

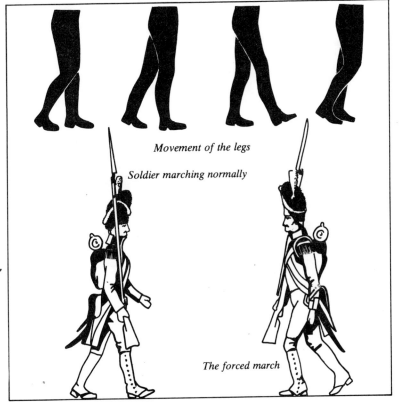

Movement of the legs

Soldier marching normally

The forced march

59

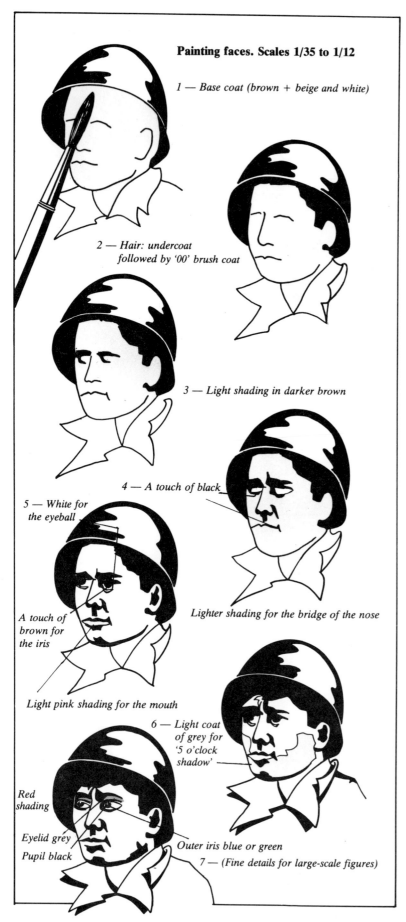

Painting faces. Scales 1/35 to 1/12

1 — Base coat (brown + beige and white)

2 — Hair: undercoat followed by '00' brush coat

3 — Light shading in darker brown

4 — A touch of black

5 — White for the eyeball

Lighter shading for the bridge of the nose

A touch of brown for the iris

Light pink shading for the mouth

6 — Light coat of grey for '5 o'clock shadow'

Red shading

Eyelid grey

Pupil black

Outer iris blue or green

7 — (Fine details for large-scale figures)

Choosing your Paints and knowing how to use them

The experts argue endlessly about the qualities of different paints. There are those who will not hear of acrylics, others swear by them. In practice, acrylics used on figures give the best results when you take into consideration how easy they are to use. In fact people who do a lot of modelling find that water-colours and acrylics can be used together; indeed, they can be mixed. Water-colour gives a completely non-shiny look, lifeless even; while acrylic has a slight sheen to it. Using them together you can get every gradation of shine or flatness. On its own, acrylic is suitable for leather, fur and hair. Mixed with water-colour, it can be used for skin, wood and metal. Water-colour alone is suitable for cloth.

Everything we are saying here for figures applies equally well to vehicles, scenery, aeroplanes. We must make reservations with respect to oil paints. These are not easy to use and the beginner should certainly not even try. Acrylic, on the other hand, spreads efficiently and dries rapidly, and where accuracy of colour is not all-important, ranges of easy-to-use vinyl-acrylic paints are available. They mix with water and are particularly suitable for figures.

Use your finger to rub down relief details with a lighter tint (the basic paint with a 'bloom' of white and thinner)

Areas to be painted darker than the real thing (using a '00' brush)

Details of clothing

How to paint figures

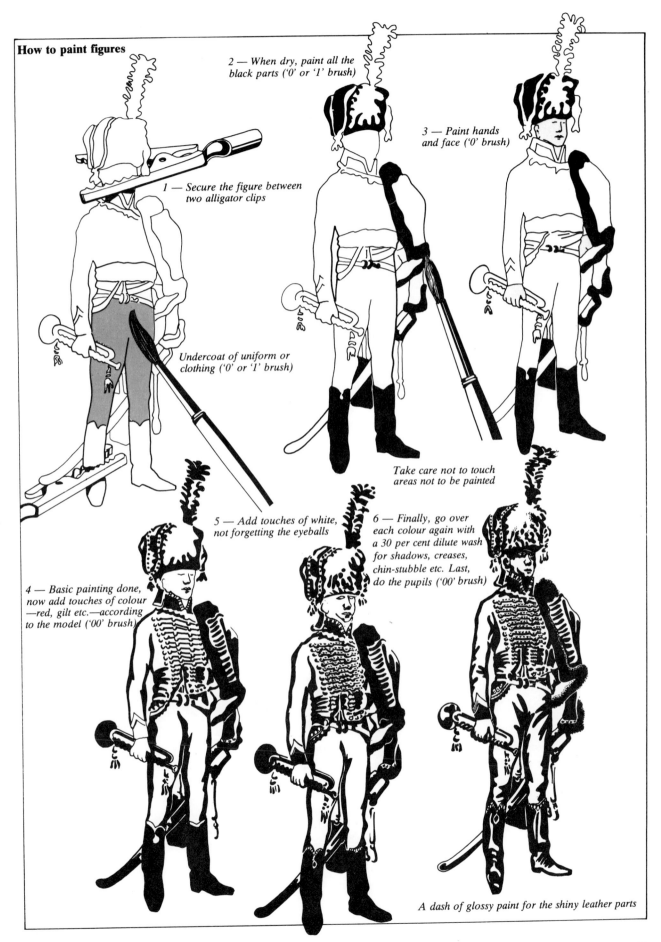

2 — When dry, paint all the black parts ('0' or '1' brush)

3 — Paint hands and face ('0' brush)

1 — Secure the figure between two alligator clips

Undercoat of uniform or clothing ('0' or '1' brush)

Take care not to touch areas not to be painted

5 — Add touches of white, not forgetting the eyeballs

6 — Finally, go over each colour again with a 30 per cent dilute wash for shadows, creases, chin-stubble etc. Last, do the pupils ('00' brush)

4 — Basic painting done, now add touches of colour —red, gilt etc.—according to the model ('00' brush)

A dash of glossy paint for the shiny leather parts

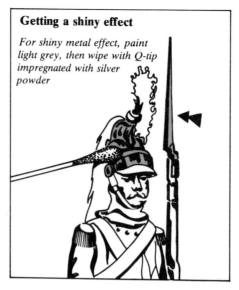

Getting a shiny effect

For shiny metal effect, paint light grey, then wipe with Q-tip impregnated with silver powder

Painting Horses

A tableau or a diorama with people in it also needs accessories. The horse counts as an accessory, in that he is almost always present in scenes of events that happened before the year 1900, but horses, along with other animals, are almost as difficult to paint well as they are to draw. A horse is not the same colour all over. The underside and hindquarters have lighter fur than the back. When you are painting horses, to avoid mistakes you must refer to books and postcards. A grey horse, for instance, is usually dappled. The direction of the hair plays an important part in what a horse looks like. Model-makers who want to create scenes with numbers of horses should refer to the work of Monsieur Leliepvre of the Historex company. He has made an exhaustive study of ways to paint horses.

Present-day Scenes with Figures

While there is an enormous choice of figures for making historical tableaux, modern figures are mostly soldiers from 1939–45. Civilians and famous people of our time are occasionally available in metal alloy. All the techniques of assembling and painting the figures are the same as for the historical kind. Tamyia, Heller, Esci, and Preiser make figures on the following scales: 1/9, 1/25, 1/35 and 1/72. On the smaller scales, a human figure

Assembly of horses

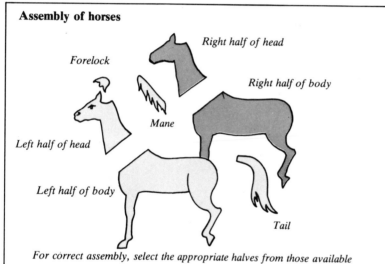

Forelock

Right half of head

Right half of body

Left half of head

Mane

Left half of body

Tail

For correct assembly, select the appropriate halves from those available

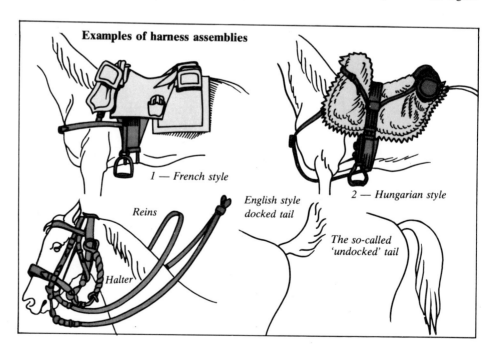

Examples of harness assemblies

1 — French style

2 — Hungarian style

English style docked tail

Reins

Halter

The so-called 'undocked' tail

really only acts as a realistic touch for the model that he is in. Details cannot really be achieved at 1/90 or 1/35. Modern figures, no matter what the scale, have one great advantage: they can be part of a scene that is simply full of things—vehicles, aeroplanes, military and civilian accessories, outdoor scenery.

The Surrounding Scenery

In the fourth part of this book, we shall deal with scenery in general. In the narrower field of settings for figures, we shall confine ourselves to general atmosphere since the scenery will always be large-scale—a street corner, a room, an inn, a forest clearing.

A small tableau with figures can be 20 to 25cm and 45 to 60cm long. At 1/25 and 1/35 the number of figures can vary from 10 to 15. You can buy various accessories as 'props'—crockery, furniture, lamps—as well as basic scenery blocks which you can paint. The rest is left up to the artist's imagination.

For scenes that happen indoors, the ground is left flat; while for exterior scenes (see part 4 of this book) it is slightly inclined. With an interior scene, the ceiling slopes. As in a drawing, all planes above the theoretical horizon line should be angled so that they would converge. It is easy to do. Just make a sketch on a piece of drawing paper, the same size as the tableau. Extend the lines on the sketch to the vanishing point, and apply them to the three-dimensional model. A few pencil strokes will provide guide-lines. Following the sketch, the entire scene will be built on the principle of 'trompe l'oeil', or false perspective. Only the vertical lines will remain unchanged.

You must decide where in the scene to place each figure. Having decided, take a sharp point or a pin, heat it, and stick it into the base or the foot of the figure. The plastic will melt and re-harden. This will ensure a perfect join between the figure and the ground of your tableau. You should also make a tiny hole in the ground

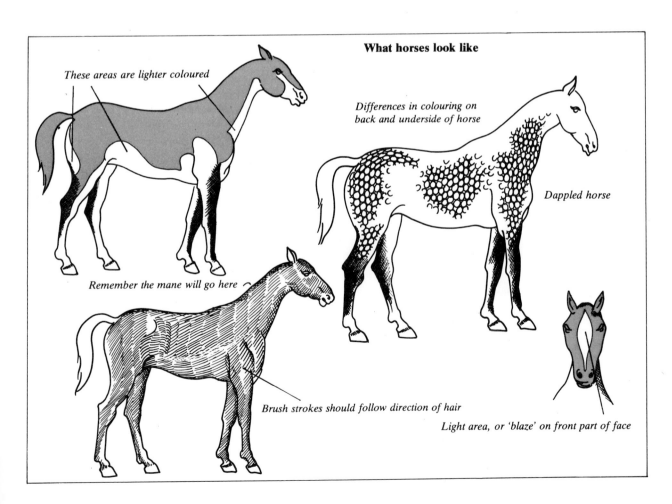

What horses look like

These areas are lighter coloured

Differences in colouring on back and underside of horse

Dappled horse

Remember the mane will go here

Brush strokes should follow direction of hair

Light area, or 'blaze' on front part of face

for the pin. This procedure eliminates the need for pedestals and gives your figures stability. The ground can be made of cardboard or anything else. Avoid trying to make tile floors because the perspective problems will drive you mad! The use of pressed cardboard for bricks, walls and tiles makes the work easier but, if possible, its natural shininess should be dulled by a coat of paint.

For small exterior scenes, relief features can be made with paper mixed with cellulose or glue, well mashed-up to make a malleable putty. Finishing can be done with a vinyl or cellulose coating, which is far more practical than traditional plaster.

When positioning your accessories, your vehicles (see below) and your figures, do not squash them together and do not scatter them too widely—both of these things are equally to be avoided. Finally,

do not forget that a tableau in a glass case will only be seen from one side, so place your figures accordingly.

Special Paints for Figures
Besides the matt and gloss paints available for different kinds of models, there are paints specially developed for use on lead or plastic figures. They enable colours on models to come very close to looking like the real thing. Their exact hues were selected after consultation with braid-makers, the textile industry, dyers and military tailors. There are some fifty shades for figures, as well as a certain number of standard contemporary military colours (Afrika Korps, fieldgrey, khaki). There is also a range of special colours for horses.

...and other items
You can finish off your figures successfully if you have everything you need. Apart from paints, there are special cloths for the flocking of figures (see the chapter on Scenery for Flocking). They come in black, blue, white, red, green, brown and yellow. There is also fine leather for making shoulder belts, saddlebags and saddles. Although we mention these materials here because they are essential for painting figures, they are useful for other models too.

Deciding whether to 'Age' your Figures
In the course of this book we shall come across various ways of 'ageing' models. With figures, it may be a question of making them look as though they belong to a particular era, rather than actually making them look old. In the same way, a photograph or a postcard can look weighed down by the years. Soldiers at Waterloo or Monte Cassino shouldn't look spick and span! If you have used oil paint on your figures, let it dry completely and then apply a further (diluted) coat. You might use, for example, a drop of tri-chloroethylene, or acetone and a little brown paint. Try it out on a piece of paper. If it's transparent, but quite visible, the mixture is right. Paint it on the figures. This will give him a 'patina'. Then wipe the relief features. With water-colours, the same effect can be achieved simply by going over him with a brush dipped in water.

GOOD

Area of secondary attraction   *Area of principal attraction*   *Uniform area of secondary importance*

POOR

No area of principal attraction: the eye wanders

Some details of the amazing 1932 Alfa-Romeo: the dashboard and the real leather upholstery. It was in an Alfa like this that Cortese and Guidotti came second at Le Mans in 1932. Luigi Fusi, the Alfa-Romeo historian, redesigned the car for Pocher.

To make scenes with figures, positions of horses and humans must be carefully studied. This is an extra exercise for the model-maker, who must 'feel' the movement of his characters.

Shown on these two pages is one of the most remarkable models to appear in recent years: the 1932 Alfa-Romeo (scale 1/8). A dash-board switch lights the headlamps. All moving parts actually work, but don't go for this one unless you are very patient. Of Italian origin and made by Pocher, this kit fascinates model-makers the world over. The lower photograph shows engine details (8 cylinders, 2.3 litres on the original). Note the fine details, including real piano hinges.

Details of the Art Collection Auto Bugatti 51. A handsome piece, much sought after by collectors since only a few were made, a reproduction of the famous blue record breaking car of 1927–31.

Making and Displaying Cars

We really ought to have said 'vintage cars' because, apart from modern racing and sports cars, vintage cars are the main interest. There are plastic and metal models available in all kinds of scale. We shall deal with the miniature ones later on—from 1/43 to about 1/72, which are the same sizes as normal toys.

The most widely available models are obtainable in the following scales: 1/18 (Hubley), 1/24 (Monogram), 1/25 (⟨ 'T) and 1/32 (Revell, Hobby Kit). There are a few rare makes available in large scales, such as the Triumph and Alfa-Romeo (by Fulgurex, Pocher, and Heller), and some more recent models like the Tamyia Datsuns at 1/12.

The Models Available

About fifteen years ago, about all you could find were construction kits for 1900–10 cars (the model-T Ford, Mercer etc.). Many of these models are no longer available today. Some of them reappear occasionally, at the whim of a manufacturer or an importer. In their 1975 catalogue, Hobby Kit announced a beautiful 1912 Hispano Suiza, a 1910 Buick, a 1908 Lanchester, a 1911 steam-powered Stanley, a 1915 Ford, the 1913 Rolls Royce and a Packard—all at 1/32.

Cars of the 1928–40 vintage are less rare than the older models. All, or nearly all, are based on American cars—1930–4 Ford and Chevrolets (Hobby Kit), or classics which we list here:

various different Duisenbergs, the Bugatti Royale, the Packard landau and saloon, Rolls Royce, the Lincoln Continental, Cadillac, Mercedes, all 1930–40 vintage (made by Monogram, Hobby Kit and Johan).

These are high-quality models, and they lend a certain uniformity to a collection. Having put together a good number of them ourselves, we are able to say that they have no major defects in moulding, and that assembly poses no insurmountable problems—except perhaps with respect to working steering wheels, on the Duisenberg in particular, which never last for very long.

'Drag' and 'street' machines must be dealt with separately—as must 'hot rods', which have their own slightly crazy corner. A company like Monogram offers about twenty different models, but for the serious model-maker, these rather far-out models can be used as a basis for building a highly personalized car. It is rather like someone who restores antiques searching the markets for the one piece missing.

Choosing from what is available, one can find the exact parts for, or come very close to, the following models:

1955 Chevrolet, Simca 5 (using a Hobby-Fiat kit), 1957 Chevrolet Corvette, Volkswagen Cub, various Ford pick-ups (1932, 1934, 1936 and 1940), 1930 and 1932 Ford cabriolets, and 1936 and 1938 Ford coupés and cabriolets. We would point out to those who are really bitten that it ought to be possible to make a 1938 Renault Celtaquatre with the parts of a 1936 Ford. There's a certain family resemblance....

And what about Metal Car Construction Kits?

These are dealt with here, because the selection of models is not very great—various 1930–2 Fords and Chevrolets, a Packard and a Duisenberg, all at 1/20. They are generally less well made than cars made entirely out of plastic. This remark does not, however, apply to large-scale models made out of both materials. The parts are moulded, so they have to be filed and then smoothed. Be that as it may, assembly is extremely easy since it is done with screws of three different sizes. The number of parts is also limited, there being no more than thirty or forty. Painting is done just as for any metal, after removal of grease with trichloroethylene. The notes that follow below, dealing with improvements to model cars, apply equally to 1/20 models. One overall difference is that detailed work is easier on the latter. We would not really advise modelmakers to use acrylic paint on matt surfaces, or matt paints on the underside of a chassis, a soft-top, or material etc.

Cars of the 1950s

Certain manufacturers have brought back easy-to-assemble models of 1949–53 cars, including Fords, Chevrolets, Mercurys, Lincolns and various English and Italian cars. They are easy to assemble, and sufficiently accurate that you will not be disappointed. Another advantage is that there are enough of them to start a collection, but what a pity they are not all on the same scale! Among the best large-scale models of the 1950s are the '49 Ford, the Mercury of the same year, and the 1950 Chevrolet coupé.

Choosing the Colour for your Model Cars

Sometimes manufacturers sell car models roughly the same colour as the real thing, but usually this is only the colour of the moulded plastic and, of course, you should not just use any old colour on any old car.

The Period 1920–60

Before the appearance of the first black closed car when Ford went into mass production, cars were gaily coloured—green, red, blue—black being a supplementary colour only. From 1925 to 1940, cars mass-produced in Europe had rather gloomy colours: basically black, navy blue, 'gosling green', Prussian blue, sea-green, bordeaux, and chocolate. Only sports cars came in lighter colours—almond green, light green, sandy-grey and dove-grey in

France. In the United States, all colours were used from 1936, with a predominance of white and metallic hues—bright metallic green and metallic blue. Some enthusiasts had blood-coloured or garnet-red cars. The predominant colours of English cars were dark green or midnight blue. In Germany they were frequently metallic grey-green or grey, and sometimes dark green.

After the war and until 1950, black remained the predominant colour in France. Blue-greys, light greens and beiges then began to appear. 1956–60 saw the two-tone fashion for cars in western countries, although they first appeared in the States in 1951. In the States from 1955–60 the colours ran riot—violet, lilac, sulphur yellow, apple green—and Europe followed suit almost at once. It is worth noting that model cars can be sprayed with genuine car paint (black in particular), provided a suitable undercoat is used first to help it adhere properly.

Interior Upholstery etc.

From 1920 to about 1940, sports cars had leather interiors—black, brown, beige, red or blue, depending on the car. 1920–30 limousines were almost always done in grey or beige material. Dark tan velvet first appeared around 1932 and made car interiors look rather gloomy. Colours got brighter just before the war and interiors became light brown, rich red (material or leather), or light beige.

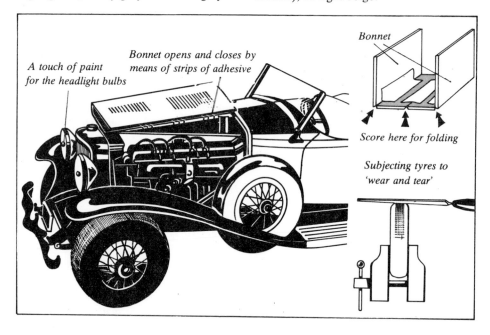

A touch of paint for the headlight bulbs

Bonnet opens and closes by means of strips of adhesive

Bonnet

Score here for folding

Subjecting tyres to 'wear and tear'

Giving a 'vintage' look to a vintage model

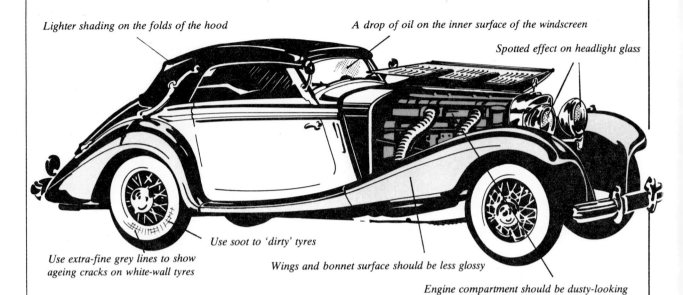

Lighter shading on the folds of the hood

A drop of oil on the inner surface of the windscreen

Spotted effect on headlight glass

Use soot to 'dirty' tyres

Use extra-fine grey lines to show ageing cracks on white-wall tyres

Wings and bonnet surface should be less glossy

Engine compartment should be dusty-looking

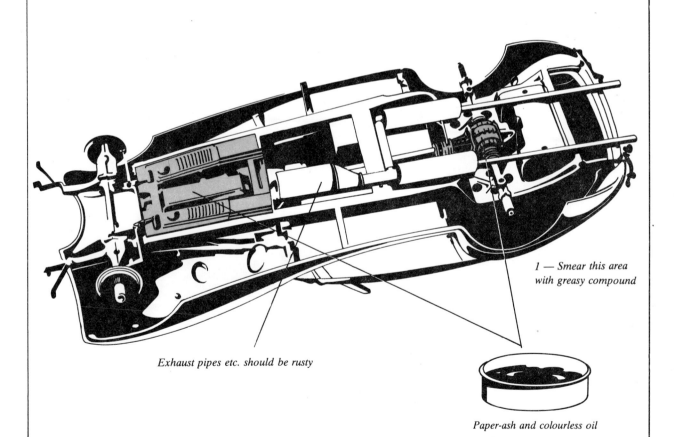

1 — Smear this area with greasy compound

Exhaust pipes etc. should be rusty

Paper-ash and colourless oil

1

2

1930–50—the Golden Age of the Automobile. Cars of this period yield the most exciting models. (1) The underside of an Alfa. (2) A Bugatti, the most amazing car of all time. Most scale-model companies are interested in it. The 1932–3 Bugatti could reach 110mph (175kph). (3) An 812 Cord, little known in Europe. The first American front-wheel-drive car. A real collector's item. (4), (5) and (6) The vintage car model-maker adds the finishing touches with the help of photographs, taken in museums and exhibitions, to which he can refer. (7) Interior finishing can be difficult, involving considerable dexterity—micro stitching, for example! Take your choice.

3

4

Making Improvements to 1930–50 Models

We have chosen this particular period because the cars of that time have a number of points in common: bodywork is always done in glossy monochrome, occasionally in two-tone from about 1950, and the tyres are often white-walled. From 1946 onwards, separate wings with running-boards disappeared, making way for the streamlined look. The wings were absorbed into the body proper. Convertibles are particularly attractive as interior details can be worked on more easily.

5

6

7

Windows, doors and openings: The accessories that come with kits are often too large and difficult to position. They can be replaced by thin pieces of rhodoid, as we shall see in the case of small cars. Sun visors are frequently omitted from lists of necessary accessories. Carpeting of the interior of a car can be done either with material or with blotting-paper that has been dipped into acrylic paint of the right colour. Between 1930 and 1950, car interiors were almost always either beige or brown.

Some experts change fixed doors into doors that open. This is a long and ticklish job. All the moulding in the hinge end of the door has to be worked on with the pointed X-Acto tool. When you have almost cut through it, hold the inside of the door over an alcohol lamp (about 15cm above it) to soften it, and continue cutting. Once there is an opening, you can continue with a jeweller's saw. You must then either replace the carpeting or alter it, and then make hinges and joints with extra bits of plastic. An easier but less robust answer is to use double-sided adhesive tape. Cut rubber sealing strips

out of black drawing paper and glue them into the space left empty between door and bodywork. There should be between 1/4 and 1/2cm play. This technique can also be used for convertible hoods and rear boot-lids. With four-door models, we do not recommend making them all operational, as this will tend to weaken the body generally.

Finally, the real 'nut' who wants roll-down windows can do it as follows: if the car has window-handles, make a hole in the inside of the door. Cut an eccentric circle out of cardboard. Slide this down between the two halves of the door. With a pin fix the handle in line with the hole in the door, and catch the cardboard too. It may not work for ever, but turning the handle ought to raise and lower the piece of rhodoid cut in the shape of a window.

Interior: The major defect of most instructions is that they tell you to use the same colour throughout. In fact, when you look inside a car, metal, wood and material have very different reflections and textures. Usually the plastic pieces representing chrome are too big (mirror,

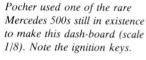

Pocher used one of the rare Mercedes 500s still in existence to make this dash-board (scale 1/8). Note the ignition keys.

window-handles, door-handles, buttons, air-vents etc.). Rather than cutting them down to their correct size, proceed as follows. Take hold of each piece in an alligator clip—or, before cutting it off from its 'tree', redraw it with a thin black paint line. This applies especially to wind-screen wipers: paint the blades black with a '00' brush (the rubber part), and the arms silver-grey.

Between 1930 and 1938, American cars had dash-boards made of painted metal, shiny or matt, so few or no changes are necessary. From 1939 to 1942, and from 1946 to 1950, imitation wood was used. To get this effect, paint the whole dash-board brown ('0' brush) and then, with a '00', give a few tiny touches of beige and shiny bright chestnut-colour. Follow this with a gloss coat (cream paint mixed equally with thinner), and finally a light varnish to make the whole thing shine. Still on dash-boards, remember that switches and buttons were made of an almost yellow-coloured ivory plastic. Carpeting is painted as follows: a thick undercoat, then deeper overpainting in the folds and lighter touches on the prominent parts. All the techniques of painting clothing mentioned earlier apply equally to the interior decor of cars.

Engine and mechanical parts: Apart from a few details like the radiator motif, the distributor head, the battery and the heating system, everything should be painted in matt colours. Here too we want to see variations in greys and beiges, according to dustiness, age, or simple reflection of light. Varieties of electrical wiring can be done in sewing-thread (black), impregnated with liquid transparent glue to give it substance. Thin electric wire, of the kind used for electric trains or for large-scale electric models, is suitable for the various water-pipes and hoses. Plastic housings and sheeting that seem over-sized (underneath the car, for example) can be replaced by $223g/m^2$ drawing paper (stout). Finally, screws and bolts can be represented by a little touch of silver paint mixed equally with acetone to give it a matt appearance.

Modifications to Cars or Lorries

We are entering now the realms of art and high technique. We are talking, for example, of making a one-off model from a standard kit, a convertible from a saloon car, or vice-versa, or a vehicle that was adapted and used in the 1939–45 war. In those days, model-makers started with

Next page: Models of two celebrated 1939–45 wartime vehicles, the Opel Blitz half-track, and the Russian Gaz rocket-launcher. The Gaz was a modification of the American 1942 GMC, and the Opel (affiliated to General Motors) was based on the 1936–7 Chevrolet—a strange reconciliation!

At bottom of page: A modern American long-distance truck.

71

many vintage models that can be much modified. However, certain military transport vehicles can be successfully altered to look like post-war vehicles; for example, the Opel Blitz (Italerei, scale 1/35) from the Horch KF215 (1/35). Incidentally this model may be used as a foundation for the famous Russian all-terrain GAZ. Another example: the Krauss-Maffei 8-ton artillery transporter, which can be made into a truck (Italerei and Tamyia). The Monogram 2.5 GMC, the 1/72 Esci 4 X 4 Dodge, the 4 X 4 Horch, the Chevrolet 30-cwt and the Esci 1/72 Opel Blitz—these are all considered useful foundations, or as sources of replacement parts for civilian models.

Materials to Use

Modifications involving only plastic present no real problems if it is only a question of cutting, opening, shaping, shortening or narrowing. On the other hand, adding material is rather more tricky. If a model is to be transformed, first set aside the pieces. Make a preliminary assembly of the body and the chassis with little bits of adhesive tape. Then on drawing paper or, even better, on graph paper, project vertically and horizontally the overall dimensions of the pieces to be joined. Using this drawing, now make a tracing from which you can make either the finished piece or a matrix. Use the matrix to make a preliminary shape in modelling clay. (For example, the interior of a car that was originally a convertible). Although only provisional, and in need of final shaping and smoothing, this model will serve as a guide. Apply special damp moulding paper to it. When dry, the mould conforms to what you made by hand. Remove the matrix and the clay and adjust the new shell to correspond to the old. Scissors will be needed for the first adjustment. The piece that results should be dampened with a brush to avoid fluffiness and then polished two or three times. Once you have got it right, glue it into position.

rather accurate toys (the Chevrolet truck sold by Vebe) to make ordinary trucks into gas-tankers. At one time they used 'Miror' cans for these tankers. Nowadays the great variety of equipment available to the model-maker enables him to make all sorts of different commercial vehicles. Trucks with people in them, taxis, rally cars, publicity vehicles or period scenes—they are all reasons for modifying kits. Re-reading magazines like 'Touring-Club' and 'l'Illustration' of 1930−40, or 'l'Automobile' of 1946−8, one gleams precious ideas and information about particular characteristics of the cars and lorries of the day.

A Fund of Replacement Parts

As far as utility vehicles go, there are not

To make the parts of a vehicle that are not cast or pressed metal, you can use drawing paper, cardboard, or a plastic compound like Body Putty, and even ready-made U, T and L-shapes. These may be metal (see glossary of products) or plastic. They help for example in reconstructing a chassis. Strips of wood (poplar, mahogany, balsa) will do for planks, boards or tool boxes. To make tonneau-covers and tarpaulins, first fashion a little supporting frame in thin metal wire (preferably brass as it is the most supple), straightening it out with pliers and soldering on one or two cross-pieces as necessary. Now cover this frame with gauze, moist blotting-paper, or silk—already painted the desired colours.

If you use blotting-paper, be sure to stretch it well so that it hugs the frame while drying. We recommend indelible paint beforehand, so that the whole thing can then be soaked to ensure close fitting.

Using the real thing—material, leather, metal, wood, which all have a certain thickness—is only a good idea with large-scale models (at least 1/16). Apart from anything else, these materials cause ungainly imbalances of volume. That is why we commend paper, thin strips of wood, and fine substances such as gauze.

Ballast — A Useful Trick

All plastic models without exception have one fault which is at the same time an advantage: they are too light. A model may be beautifully painted and finished, but it is a disappointment when you pick it up. So the addition of ballast, to create an illusion of weight, seems a good idea. Ballasting must be planned at the same time as assembly. The instructions tell you how to join all the components, one by one—and of course there will be empty spaces. Two very common substances can be used as ballast: household filler or modelling clay. For example, to a model weighing 100gm (experiment done on a 1/35 1936 Ford made by Monogram), we added 80 to 100gm of ballast. By doubling the weight of the vehicle, we gave it a real 'metallic' feel. This is useful for tractors, tanks, guns, cars or motorcycles. It is superfluous for aeroplanes, because you never expect them to feel heavy anyway! Take care that the ballast is well hidden and evenly distributed. Soldering wire, or fuse wire inserted into long components, with clay wrapped round it, will add weight to a chassis or a cross-piece. Of course, ballasting is only worthwhile for models which may one day be picked up.

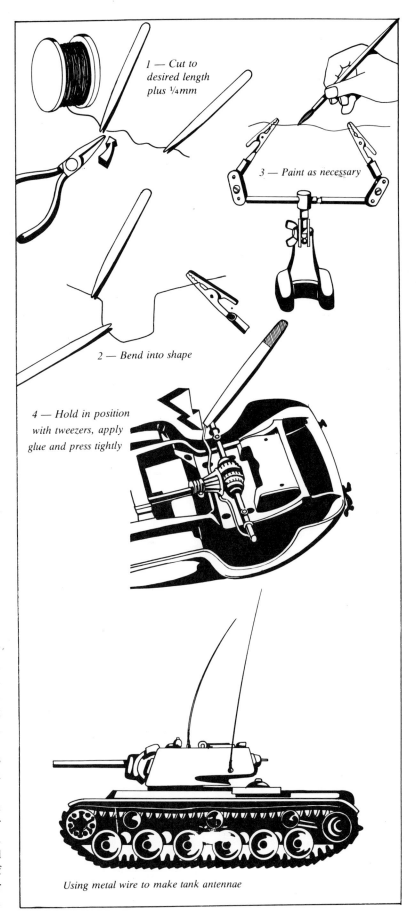

1 — Cut to desired length plus ¼mm

3 — Paint as necessary

2 — Bend into shape

4 — Hold in position with tweezers, apply glue and press tightly

Using metal wire to make tank antennae

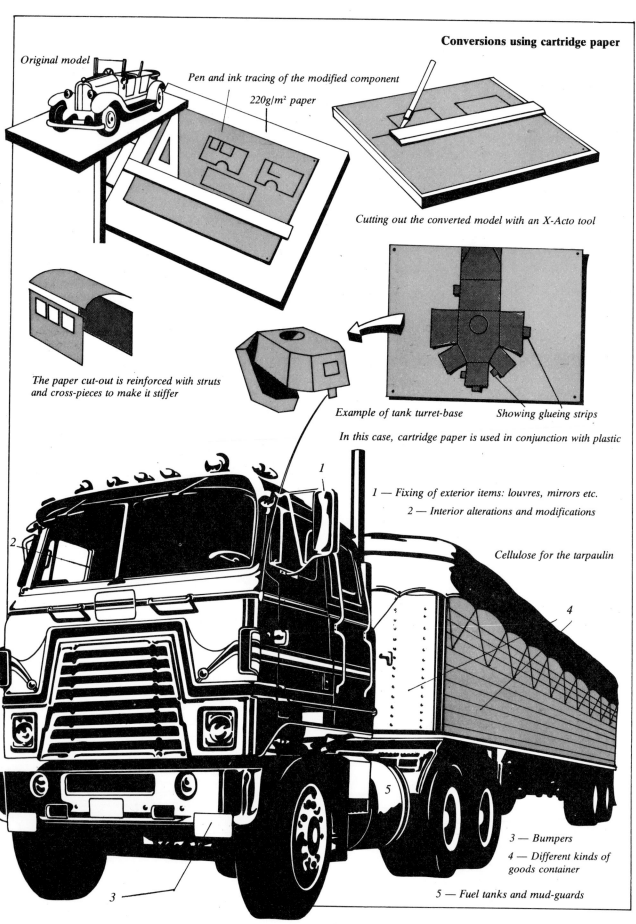

Original model

Pen and ink tracing of the modified component

220g/m² paper

Cutting out the converted model with an X-Acto tool

The paper cut-out is reinforced with struts and cross-pieces to make it stiffer

Example of tank turret-base

Showing glueing strips

In this case, cartridge paper is used in conjunction with plastic

1 — *Fixing of exterior items: louvres, mirrors etc.*

2 — *Interior alterations and modifications*

Cellulose for the tarpaulin

3 — *Bumpers*

4 — *Different kinds of goods container*

5 — *Fuel tanks and mud-guards*

Scale-model making can be an excellent introduction to engineering, not to mention a lesson in humility: given a chance, mechanics of forty years ago performed miracles. Here, a detail of the pre-1940 Mercedes 500s 8-cylinder-in-line overhead-valve engine.

Displaying Scale-Models of Cars

Everything we have said about displaying miniature cars (1/43 to 1/72) applies to models between 1/25 and 1/32, provided you have room. In general, you will be restricted to fairly restrained scenes: the end of a race, a garage on Sunday evening, a stand at the motor show. Glass-case display is also very attractive. With medium-sized models, one can add a bit of window-dressing. Take a frame of the kind used to display butterflies and decorate the inside. Place the model car in it, plus one or two accessories, such as a bench, a lamp or a human figure. This will make for an exquisite little tableau. Eight or ten of these in a room can have a beautiful effect.

Improving on and Transforming Miniature Vehicles

Over the last twenty-five years there have been enormous improvements with regard to the accuracy and the finish of miniatures, toy cars and other vehicles. Some of them indeed are so lifelike that young and not-so-young collectors do not hesitate to enthuse over them.

Models on the Market

There are so many makes that it would be foolish to try to list them all, but certain broad categories emerge from the ranges available. The most common scale of all is 1/43, which corresponds to the '0' class in model railways. On this scale, a human figure works out at about 3.5cm tall. There are also some models at 1/50 and 1/72. These are usually trucks, plant vehicles or military machines. As far as precision is concerned, there seems to be a certain anarchy abroad because the same model, supposed to be on the same sclae, some-times varies as much as 15 to 20 per cent in its dimensions. The basic categories, both for collecting and for making into other things, are these:
—production and sports cars;
—racing and rally cars;
—military and armoured vehicles;
—fire engines;
—vintage cars;
—trucks;
—plant vehicles.
Each class has its own particular problems of research and compatibility. Many tech-niques that apply to the 'large' models (1/8, 1/16, 1/35) can be used on these standard products but, at the same time, certain special cases do arise.

Information and Documentation

Before modifying a present-day vehicle, you need brochures and technical publica-tions concerning the vehicle. For cars and trucks, simple magazines and maintenance guides should suffice. For military equip-ment and plant vehicles, you must refer to highly specialized publications. In the case of vintage cars, there are various bookshops equipped to supply model-makers with diagrams and old maintenance and repair guides.

Modifying Bodywork and Chassis

1/48 models are made of two ingredients—zamak (a zinc and aluminium alloy), and injected plastic. Like any soft alloy, zamak can be drilled and sawn. Thus a saloon car can be converted into a convertible without major difficulty. Cutting-down can always be done with a fine-toothed saw and a soft triangular file. Finishing is done with emery paper. Mouldings, beadings, handles and bolts on the original are some-times too hidden to make any visual difference, and sometimes forgotten because they posed moulding problems. There is a special knack to etching. First, the surface must be thoroughly scraped and cleaned. Apply a thin coat of varnish to the metal or plastic. On this use a pencil to trace the shape to be etched. Then, with a hard cutting-tool, go over the pencilled outline so as to leave a small furrow in the surface. Remove the film of varnish. Only the scooping out now remains to be done. Take a triangular-pointed tool. This kind of modification is always easier on metal than on plastic. Metal surfaces must always be cleaned with trichloroethylene, both before and after. Shop-bought models can be improved as follows: Make the doors and windows slightly smaller, and file down and polish any pieces that are too large.

Windows and openings: The rather thick pieces of plastic used nowadays can well be replaced by thin rhodoid. There is no problem cutting this with an ordinary blade. On a screw-jointed model, you have only to undo the various parts of the bodywork to get at the transparent compo-nents. In other cases, you will have to dis-mantle and be prepared to re-assemble the bodywork. Remove the original windows and lay them on top of the rhodoid, to enable accurate cutting with a blade or sharp scissors. Use tweezers and a drop of glue to fix.

Wheels: Although there have been great advances in moulding, the wheels of all miniature vehicles can do with improve-ment. The areas which are to remain chromed should be masked with Maskol. Paint the remaining parts with matt paint. The tyres (previously removed) should be given a light coat of thinner to make them more matt-looking. Wipe off immediately afterwards and examine the effect, as they are not always made of the same materials. Always use a '00' or an '0' brush to paint wheel details.

Grip the model in a small vice. Apply paint with the right-hand in thin layers, turning the rim on its axis with the left-hand (thumb or index finger). This enables you to work to within a tenth of a millimetre. Another method is to fit the axle onto a mini-drill, which can then be turned as light touches of paint are applied. This method works for tyres as well as for the wheels themselves.

With elaborately-moulded wheels, start off with a dark undercoat, going on to lighter touches.

Interiors: All sorts of improvements can be made in this area. Cushions, seats and upholstery should all be painted a matt shade, as well as the carpeting and upholstery on the insides of the doors. A better floor covering will result if you use a cartridge paper cut-out—which can also be used for the mirror and sun-visors. Dashboard painting should be done with a '00' brush.

There was something fascinating about the Bugatti dash-boards—especially the touring model's, which deserves special attention. Heller's 15TA Citroën, a newcomer in the large-scale range, is both handsome and accurate, and made entirely of plastic. The thousands of Citroën fans will be pleased. Note the bonnet raised to reveal the large 6 cylinder 78 x 100 engine developing 77hp. This car continued to be made, unchanged, from 1939 to 1954.

Exterior accessories: Unlike most models you can buy, cars are seldom all one colour. More detail will be added if you paint joints, hinges and radiator grille in a light matt grey. Wings and mudguards can be the same colour as the bodywork, but matt not glossy. On large vehicles, you can add piano or copper wire under the chassis for the various pipe and leads. Larger pipes can be made from the kind of plastic tubing used for washing-lines. Finally, windscreen-wipers can be made from extra-thin copper or brass wire.

Military vehicles — a special case: All the techniques suggested for plastic models can, of course, apply equally to military vehicles. A few points of detail to note: tarpaulins and other coverings can be replaced by or covered with pieces of fine silk painted camouflage colours, and a radio antenna can be made from a suitably painted synthetic broom-bristle. Camouflage netting can be made of painted crêpe. Military tools (shovels, pick-axes etc.) can be drawn on cartridge paper, cut out, and glued in the right positions. Home-made accessories generally need to be added: maintenance-catches, reflectors, convoy lights etc. You can buy (at 1/72) adhesive or transfer lettering for tanks and aeroplanes. Either can also be used effectively on other military vehicles.

Facing page 80:
Above: Alfa-Romeo racing car.
Below: Mack articulated truck for transporting trees. Note the boom and wheel assembly on the rear of the truck. A fine piece of modern equipment.

Page 80: Details of the Heller 1950−1 15TA Citroën. Note the accuracy of the dashboard accessories, and the fine tread on the Michelin tyres. This 1/8 model is 59cm long, 22cm wide, and has 1061 separate components.

Museums are a unique source of information for the model car enthusiast. These pictures were taken at the Saint-Dizier museum, France.

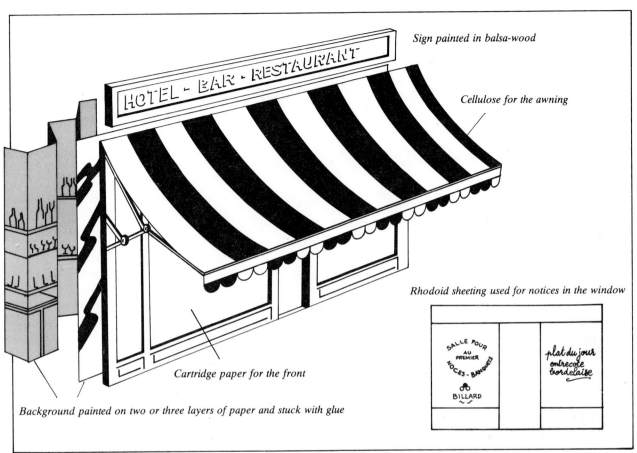

Sign painted in balsa-wood

Cellulose for the awning

Rhodoid sheeting used for notices in the window

SALLE POUR
AU
PREMIER
NOCES - BANQUETS

BILLARD

plat du jour
entrecôte
bordelaise

Cartridge paper for the front

Background painted on two or three layers of paper and stuck with glue

Final assembly of the model

Scale-model street lamp (from Brawa, Tamyia, Busch etc.)

CAFE-BAR

Figures
Bush made of foam

Scale-model

Moulded plaster for surface

1.6 to 2 times the length of the principal model

Display of 1/43 and 1/72 Models (See also chapter on Scenery)

These popular models, which you can modify yourself, have one major advantage: they do not take up much room. They can be displayed on a shelf, or in a glass case, as in a museum. You can get some twenty cars into one metre. At 1/43 you can also put together some striking little tableaux. You can obtain plastic human figures and build up a pleasing scene—for electric trains (lighting, buildings, countryside) or for any other kind of model.

We should point out, to those who want to create dioramas with perspective effects, that you can use small models in the background and 1/35 models in the foreground. A motor-race, a cross-roads at six in the evening, or a major work-site would all make good dioramas—and your imagination can take over. (See also the use of different materials for scenery). Diorama dimensions: minimum depth of 25 to 30cm; frontal length 50 to 60cm (over 100cm is too long except for very large models); height 15 to 20cm is usually enough. For a very precise small-scale scene, 20 to 25cm would do.

Models of the Past — A Brief Look

This is not supposed to be a complete and exhaustive catalogue of past models. We are keeping simply to the principal model cars made between 1939 and 1955, particularly the most common ones. To begin with they were made of zamak, not plastic.

Pre-1940

The Dinky Toys sold by Meccano were almost exactly the same as those sold after the war. Apart from the wheels, they were remarkable for their time. The Dinky range comprised a 2-seater convertible and a 4-seater convertible (similar to the Triumphs and MGs of 1935—40), a 2-door coupé and a limousine. The wheels were in white rubber. The range also included lorries on a smaller scale (about 1/80), a cattle-truck, a flat-bed truck and an Esso petrol tanker. Just before the War, Dinky added the very accurate Simca 5 and Peugeot 402 to their range. There were also taxis—blue, yellow, or two-tone cream and maroon.

(*For captions see p. 78*)

Right-hand page: The Pocher
Mercedes 500, the prestige car
of Hitler's Germany.

Scale-models which are often
ignored: tractors. Above: Two
ERTL products.
Below: The large-scale 15TA
Citroën, 1952, made by Heller.

Solido too supplied models only of contemporary cars. Their range included a touring coupé, a convertible (which worked), a saloon and a street-car—all rather American-inspired. During the War manufacture continued, although they were all blue-grey in colour.

There were certain brands—Vebe and others now forgotten—that were extremely accurate. These were quality products that were worth having: a Parisian street-car, a Renault bus and truck, on scales of about 1/35 to 1/40. Then there were the toys that were reproductions of actual vehicles, such as the Renault Viva Grand Tourer and the Celtaquatre, Citroën toys, the 3.5-ton Renault etc.

1945—65

People have been collecting the toys of this period for many years. Immediately after the War the Dinky range was enriched by a string of Ford lorries (flat-beds, tankers, rubbish trucks), and also by a handsome range of Studebaker utility trucks—in fact the models made available under the Marshall Plan. As for cars there were also a number of American models: a Packard with a driver inside, a 2-door Chrysler coupé. Then, enter the new generation of cars—the Simca Sport (1948–50), the

Peugeot 203, the Citroën 2CV etc. As well as the range of small-scale models, during the 50s Dinky also brought out industrial vehicles on a larger-scale: the Dumper, cranes, Massey Harris tractors.

So we come to the present-day. Immediately after the War, Solido continued to produce their pre-war models and added various other cars inspired by the Simca 8, the Ford Vedette and the Fiat 1400, all made between 1948 and 1952. Then they moved into larger scales—the Fregate, the Packer and the Studebaker, but these were still only toys. Around 1951-2, new brand-names started to appear—Juvaquatre, Prairie-Renault, the Renault Bulldog truck under the CIJ name. These

Facing page: Heller, Tamyia and various other companies make interesting models of Honda motorcycles. The same goes for 1939–45 military motorcycles.
Below: An ESCI BMW. Motorcycle models are generally fairly large-scale.

Below: Pocher model of the 1932 Alfa-Romeo Gran Turismo.

Pure delight: close-up of a Bugatti wheel and brake mechanism. The detail here is so subtle that we are halfway between cars and motorbikes!

handsome vehicles still turn up today in old toy-boxes. It should be noted that during the 1960s the Solido 1/43 cars came back. Remarkably well finished, they ushered miniature cars into the modern era. Today, Solido make dozens of different models. A number of new companies are reaching out toward new horizons. Their brand-names are about as numerous as their scales, which vary from 1/60 to 1/35!

1/72 Construction Kits

This scale is particularly valuable because it is the standard-scale for a lot of aeroplanes, tanks and military figures. While the choice is not vast, nevertheless with cars constructed on this scale you can make tableaux and be sure of finding everything you need for it.

Matchbox, the famous miniature toy company, brought out in 1976 a type 59 Bugatti, an SS 100 Jaguar (1930–7), and a 1931–3 Aston Martin Ulster, in addition to a range of armoured vehicles, a field in which there is huge competition. ESCI (Italy) also produce a lot of military equipment, including vehicles that can be assembled for either civilian or military tableaux—Opel trucks, the Kfz11 Half-Truck and staff cars.

Suggested Reading Matter

If you are tempted by scale-models of cars or military vehicles, you will want to know more. Modellers' supply shops carry well-informed monthly reviews which keep the model-maker up-to-date with what's going on in the world. Apart from sections on model making and what to buy, magazines carry particularly authoritative reviews telling you everything you want to know about model-making publications.

Large-Scale Model Cars

By large-scale, we mean no smaller than 1/12. These models are so detailed that: on the one hand a lot of time is needed on them, and on the other hand the techniques are very different from those we have covered so far. When undertaking a large-scale model, take your time. You will need many days or even weeks of quiet work and undisturbed evenings. It's not a question of putting together a collection efficiently, but rather of making a few handsome pieces.

The Models Available

Most components of these models are made of plastic, but certain parts are metal or rubber. The best-looking models at the moment are made by Pocher of Italy. At 1/8 they make the 130HI Fiat, the Alfa-Romeo, the Rolls Royce and the Mercedes—all pre 1938. These are large-scale models best displayed individually. For the best results, each one needs a fantastic amount of patience! Fitting the spokes on the wheels, for example, is a major operation with metal wires. It is a good idea to work in two to three hour stretches and then have a rest.

Monogram make some present-day models—an E-type Jaguar and a Corvette 65 on the same scale. These are not quite so well finished as the Pocher models, but they can be handsomely transformed and modified. There was a similar E-type Jaguar on the market about twelve years ago, very close in scale. As far as we can remember, the model we built then in 1965–6 had certain problems involving the opening of the hood and adjustment of the front suspension. The present Monogram model does not seem to have an opening boot-lid, otherwise it is very similar to the older model. Tamyia has a 1/12 Datsun

240ZG (sport) and the 240Z Safari. Interestingly, they also make human figures, accessories, tools and tyres on the same scale, which means you can put together a racing workshop or a small tableau.

While we are talking about large-scale models, we must not forget the Citroën 15TA, a handsome model which surely has a great future.

As for touring and racing cars at 1/8, the following are currently available: the Lola T70 Mk III, the 910 Carrera 10 Porsche, and a number of formula one models including the Tyrell II, the Ferrari 312, the Lotus 49B and 72D-F1, the Brabham BT44B, the Matra MS11, and so on. These monsters all come painted with the advertising of the companies that sponsored them. The quality of these models shows particularly in the elaborate detail of mechanical parts—brake-rods, shock-absorbers, pipes, nuts and bolts, all reproduced with the greatest accuracy. Assembly of these models is no more difficult than assembly of smaller-scale ones.

Assembling and Displaying Motorcycles

There are differences of manufacturing style in this field. First, there are the very small ones (Tamyia) on the classic 1/35 scale. These are designed to be part of larger scenes and to accompany other models. On a larger scale, the Protar catalogue is full of present-day motorbikes. Then come the very large-scale models put out by ESCI (1936–45 military models), Italerei (same category), Heller (present-day), and Tamyia (also present-day).

Models on the Market
The Italian company Protar and the French company Heller seem to produce the widest ranges, along with the well-established Tamyia. Protar puts out the following Italian racing machines: Morini 250, Gilera 500, MV Agusta, Mondial 250 and the Guzzi. They also make the English Norton 500 Max, and the German DKV 350 and BMW 500RS.

A characteristic of the Protar range of motorbikes is that they use both plastic and metal. Metal is used for the engines, the components of which are screwed together to assemble. Thus you get a sort of X-ray view of the engines of the BMW 500, the Side-Car, the Agusta 350, and the CZ 250 Cross. For the motorbike trials enthusiast, Protar make the Husqvarna 400 Cross, the Greeves 360 Challenger, the Montesa 247, and the MZ 250. Certain bikes in the Protar range are accurate down to the last detail. We have examined a number of different models under a magnifying glass, and these come out among the best: the Norton 750 Commando, with telescopic metal suspension, transmission chain, and entirely metal frame, not to mention cables and casings made out of the real thing; the 750 SF Laverdas, types 71 and 72; and the marvellous Moto Guzzi V.7 Special. On

all these motorbikes the engines are well reproduced, and only the dimensions of the spokes leave anything to be desired. The Vespa, so popular between 1952 and 1960, deserves special mention. (Its dimensions: 196mm long, 115mm high, 83mm wide).

So-called vintage motorcycles are made by Italerei and ESCI Polistil. They are all at 1/9. There are two German models, the BMW R.75 with side-car in the colours of Rommel's army, and the Zundapp KS 750 with or without side-car in the 1939—40 German army colours. These two models demonstrate the technical advances achieved by the Germans in their motorcycles at that time: flat twin engines with much use of aluminium mouldings, small-diameter wheels with large tyres, telescopic suspension, large drum brakes, etc. These ranges also include the English 3 HW Solo Triumph and the U.S. Army Harley-Davidson, which was the first motorbike to have a windshield. The high saddle and leather bags made it look like something out of the Wild West. The vintage machines are all handsomely made and well finished.

A Curiosity — And Present-Day Models
During the 1939—45 war, the German army used the NSU HK 101 Kettenkrad, a sort of half-track motorcycle. The only parts that were really motorcycle were the front wheel and the handlebars. The rest of it was a small tracked vehicle. The

Two vintage motorcycles: the British Triumph (above), and a Zundapp side-car (below) equipped with an M.G.42 machine-gun. On the English bike, the engine is the one used by Triumph until about 1955. Note: on the left the celebrated Sten gun used by partisans and commandos.

The Harley-Davidson against a background. Note the specially positioned saddle.

manufacturers of the scale-model have got a real one, no doubt retrieved from the western front. The Kettenkrad could carry three men and their equipment.

Tamyia make some marvellous present-day models at 1/16, including the civilian and police versions of the Harley Davidson FL H1100. Their quality leaves little to be desired, and the same is true of their various Hondas. BMWs appear more frequently than most: vintage models (1939–45) are made at 1/9, while Heller and Tamyia produce present-day models, the R 75/5, the police R 75 and the R 90 S. The only difference between the two brands is one of scale. The R 75/5, which we had occasion to build with friends, is a

real collector's item, as it takes a long time to assemble, to paint and to finish. The BMW is used by the police in Germany, Denmark, Holland, Turkey and France.

We find the 1/6 Harley Davidson somewhat easier to assemble. The manufacturers provide a very precise set of instructions which you follow step-by-step. This seems to us a better system than the old assembly diagrams.

At a scale of 1/8, Heller make the following machines: the Laverda SF and SFC, the Norton Hi-Rider and SS, with 750 engine, the Norton 750 Commando, the BMW 750, and various Hondas and Kawasakis. The 1/8 German police machine, made by Tamyia, has 350

Models of present-day motorbikes are not particularly easy to assemble. Each of the many tiny details can become a miniature masterpiece.

85

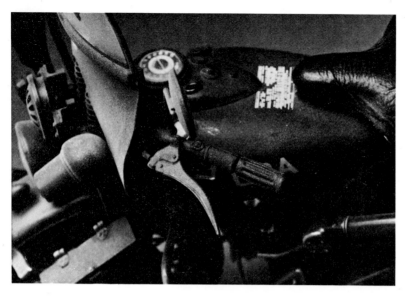

Detail of a U.S. army motor-bike, the Harley Davidson.

This 1/8 Heller model of a Laverda 750 SF motorcycle is one of a series of twelve models.

separate parts. Revell also make a number of machines at 1/8: the Kawasaki Mach III, the Harley Davidson Electra, and the Triumph Tiger. We must make particular mention of this last machine, which dates from 1952. It is a real collector's item, the only machine at the mid-point between 'vintage' motorcycles and the present-day. Revell (whose products are exported to the United States) also make various sorts of Chopper.

A Few Words About Motorcycle Construction Kits

Unlike other vehicles, motorcycles do not really lend themselves to modification or transformation. Assembling them does not require any very special know-how. They simply have to be done extremely carefully, that's all. No piece can be concealed, the slightest slip will show. Transfers must be stuck on especially carefully. This process can be helped by the addition of a drop of eau-de-Cologne or alcohol in the bowl used for soaking them; it will help the transfer to slip more easily into the correct position. A simple wipe with a sponge or chamois-leather cloth removes the surplus. More than with any other kind of model, glue must be used very sparingly. Select the most liquid kind possible, and apply it by brush. During assembly, do not be afraid to use adhesive tape to hold together pieces that have just been glued. When painting frames and other small parts, a quick and easy method is to hang each piece to be painted on a thread and use a spray-gun. Turn the piece as you paint, to achieve a uniform surface. When it comes to complicated assemblies involving several pieces, use a vice: it will save you trouble. Remember too that if you have trouble shaping plastic lines and casings correctly, they soften easily in 60–70 °C water; use pliers to obtain the desired shape and then dip them in cold water (with an ice-cube in it). This makes shaping them much easier. Otherwise, the techniques that apply to other models apply equally to motorcycles.

Constructing and Displaying Tanks

Military model making is enormously popular. Combat tanks are particularly in fashion at the moment.

For those interested in starting a collection, we have tried in this chapter to give an overall picture of the principal types made between 1939 and 1970, with an indication of the ones that are available in scale-models (sometimes toys). They are classified by nation.

Great Britain

British tanks look quite different from American tanks. There are not many 1939–45 models on the market. Tamyia market the Matilda Mk II and the Lee M.3 (1/35). The Matilda was an infantry tank designed in 1937 and 2,987 were made up to 1943. As for conversions, it is fun to use this kit to make the Matilda Scorpion with mine-protection, or the Matilda Amra Mk I–A. The Lee tank—and its opposite number the Grant, intended for the British—appeared in 1941 and was the predecessor of the famous Sherman. This tank was also built in the United States. The only difference in the English version was in the turret. At 1/72, there are models of the Valentine Mk III tank and the Churchill Mk IV built between 1941 and 1945. There is a construction kit for the A22F made in 1944. ESCI Polistil also market the Matilda. More recent English tanks are also available—the Centurion and the Chieftain, which achieved fame in Korea and the Middle East in 1973. Available in 1/72, 1/35 and 1/25.

Germany

Of all the categories of scale-models, Germany is best represented in tanks. Almost the complete range from 1940—5 can be created, as follows:
—The Panzer Kampfwagen II·(PKW II), a Tamyia model. There are scale-models of the prototypes (versions A, B and C) made between 1937 and 1939. This tank weighed 9.5 tons and had a crew of three, a 20mm canon and a 10.3mm machine-gun. By using different wheels in the tracks you can make the VK 1601 and Lynx models built in 1942.

—The PKW III. The basic Tamyia model can be converted into a number of versions that were used by the Wehrmacht—models B, D, H, J and L. The additional purchase of a PKW IV kit permits construction of all the versions of the Mk III until it stopped being produced in 1943, that is to say about fifteen editions. (There are excellent photographs for learning to tell them all apart in the book 'Tanks of

These model tanks (1/72) are in the ESCI catalogue. Although some purists consider this kind of model a hybrid, they are suitable for tableaux on small surfaces. They are also very accurate.

Above: The Panzer tank captured in 1944. For a long time it was on show at Les Invalides in Paris before being transferred to the tank museum.

Below: Contemporary AMX 30 turret (Heller). 1/35 model.

and remained so until May 1945. A 75mm canon was standard. A slightly different version, the Jagdpanzer self-propelled gun, is available on the same base-platform from Tamyia, at 1/25 and 1/36.

—The PKW VI, the Tiger, originally designed for combat on the Russian front, where it was up against those redoubtable Soviet tanks the T.34 and the KV 1. There are models on three scales—1/25 (with motor), 1/35 and 1/72.

—The PKW VI Tiger II (the Königstiger), built in November 1943. The first production models went into service a year after the prototype. Up to May 1945, 484 tanks of this type were built. They come in 1/35 and 1/72.

To make a German tank collection really complete, Heller supplies construction kits at 1/35 for tanks built since 1960—in particular the Gepard 320 P and the famous Leopard II and IV, widely considered to be the best tanks in the world, on a level with the French AMX 30 and the new American GM tanks.

France

Most manufacturers of model tanks are little interested in French tanks owing to the relatively short involvement of French armour in the 1939–40 campaigns, and the fact that all armour stationed in France from 1940 to 1945 was idle. Solido produce various 1/72 models of the principal French tanks of 1939–40—the Renault 35 and the Somua S.35. A survey of the tanks of that time of course includes the Hotchkiss B–1, D 2 and AMX 40, machines that ought to be available as scale-models, but only Heller appear to be showing any interest in producing them.

After 1945, there were basically two types of armour—the armoured scout-car and the AMX. They first appeared in 1951. There are various versions of the AMX 13 on a scale of 1/35, including the 155 self-propelled gun, tanks with 75mm and 105mm cannon, anti-aircraft gun, and the armoured personnel carrier used for troop transport.

The AMX 30, of which the first real prototype appeared in 1960, is now standard equipment in the French army. There is a 1/35 scale-model, in both combat and anti-aircraft versions. The connoisseur of French armour will notice

1915–1945', published in the United States by Galahad Books and sold in specialist bookshops and modellers' suppliers).

—The PKW IV. Up until 1943, this was the German army's most important tank. It differs in detail from the Mk III, notably in being equipped with a 75mm canon. With a 1/35 model, various different versions can be built, including the model J which appeared in 1944 and had a mounted bazooka. Model G is also available on the market. Solido make a toy version (1/72).

—The PKW V. Better known as the Panzer. The allies considered this the most effective German tank. Models of it are available in 1/25, 1/35 and 1/72 (Solido). The real machine was in service in 1942

that none of the usual armoured unit ancillary vehicles are available at present—the Berliet and Simca 5-ton trucks, Peugeot appliances, Someca trucks etc. For the beginner, there are easy-to-assemble 1/72 versions of the AMX 13 and the AMX 30.

The United States

The United States produced more tanks than any other nation during the Second World War, and is correspondingly well represented in scale-models.

—The M.3 tank, made in conjunction with the Commonwealth, known as the Lee in the U.S.A. The best known version is the M3 A2. Tamyia produce a 1/35 model.

—The M.4 tank, better known as the Sherman. A number of models (1/72, 1/43, 1/35, 1/25 and 1/16) show the various stages of development of this, the best known American tank. The most frequently reproduced are the M4 A3 and the M4 A4 (Tamyia, Airfix, Monogram etc.). (We must also make special mention of the 1/16 motorized version of the Sherman). There are various scale-model versions of the M.4, including the rocket-launcher (Monogram). A number of well-turned-out Solido 1/72 toys can be used for conversions—not only the M.4, but also the open-turret Cruiser.

—The M.3 Stuart tank, lightweight, originally equipped with a 37mm cannon and a platform for a 105mm mortar. First made in 1940. The name Stuart was used by the Commonwealth armies, and M.3 by the Americans (available in 1/35).

—Present-day tanks. A number of American tanks are available in kits—the M.60, the M.60 E1 and the Patton—in 1/72, 1/35 and 1/25.

The U.S.S.R.

Russian tanks were for a long time almost unknown to the model-maker. There are two main models available in 1/35, the famous T.34 and the K.V.1, the second less well-known than the first. It was the K.V.1 that faced the German Tiger in 1942 and 1943. The models are extremely accurate. There are other models in 1/35, including the T.44 and the K.V.85, made by converting and modifying the first two. There is also a model of the I.S.3, the later edition of the Stalin tank.

At 1/72 there are more recent tanks like the SU.100. These need a lot of conversion and finishing off.

Japan

There are kits of certain rare models used during the 1939–45 war. At 1/35, the Type 97 Shinhoto-Chi medium tank, used in operation in 1942. It was armed with a 47mm cannon and two 7.7 machine-guns. Other Japanese 1939–45 tanks are not available in scale-models. On the other hand, one can get more recent machines,

Model of the Elefant self-propelled gun. There are various models of this hybrid machine, the result of much research. The entire wheel assembly, in particular, was intended for a prototype version of the Tiger tank. The scale-model is very impressive.

such as the defensive M.B.71. This is rather similar to contemporary American and European tanks. It carries a 105mm cannon and is current Japanese army equipment.

Italy

There are plenty of Italian 1939–45 model aeroplanes around, but nothing like so many armoured vehicles. The M.13–40 is one of the few models available in 1/35 and 1/72. First used in 1940, this tank underwent numerous modifications, and by 1942 had changed a good deal. They only made 82 of the final version. The Tamyia model is the African version, while ESCI has a more European edition at 1/72.

Other Countries

There are already scale-models of Swedish tanks. By burrowing into the records of various countries and reference works on 1939–45 armour, and using the models available as a base, it is possible to turn out tanks of other nations—Czechoslovakia, Poland, Australia and Canada, whose armour had certain features in common with that of other machines. Furthermore, if you draw on historical documents you will get some idea of the spoils of war and how tanks were often converted.

Modification and Conversion of Models

Whatever the scale being used, there are a certain number of traditional tricks, including the use of transfers, that help to individualize your armour. We have gone through all the literature available and, more important, the complete range of armoured vehicles built between 1936 and 1945 (hundreds of different models). We have come to the conclusion that it is possible to build your own highly individualized models which nevertheless reproduce what was actually made. Here, country by country, are some armoured vehicles that can be put together, using what is available in the shops.

Canada

Starting out with a Sherman kit, a Grant kit, and the modified turret of a Russian K.V.1, you can make three different RAM tanks—the Mk I, Mk II, and the Command Operational Tank.

The Canadian tank was a hybrid Anglo-American/Canadian concept. It was made from 1941 to 1943. As for the Grizzly I tank, it was the Canadian version of the American M.4. The modification-conversion is not very complicated.

This 'giant' Tamyia model tank is a reproduction of one of the numerous Sherman M.4 tanks built between 1943 and 1946. This one has one of the latest wheel assemblies. This 1/16 scale-model has tread components which must be assembled one by one. Turret and motor radio-controlled. The veritable prototype of the good quality powered model.

Czechoslovakia

There are models available of the Skoda and Tatra tanks used by the Germans between 1939 and 1945. ESCI makes the T35 Skoda in 1/72. This kit will also make the ST.39, in line with actual production—300 of these tanks were made to equip the Czech army. Another piece of armoured equipment, the LT.38 (Praga TNHP), can be made by using the Marder III incorporated into the German army (ESCI kit). From 1942 onwards, Czech production was tied into German, to produce the Hetzers and Marders. The turret can be made from a Tamyia M.13–40, while the chassis is that of a Panzer I.

Germany

The various 1/35 models available make it possible to construct the various versions that were actually built between 1937 and 1943, starting with the Mk III and the Mk IV. Using Panzer models, the various versions can be made, including the D.1, the D.2, the A, and even the observation tank (the Beobachtungspanzer) with fixed turret and gun, used by artillery officers. The platform of the Elefant self-propelled gun (available in various brands) can take a Tiger turret to produce the P prototype of this tank (dating from 1942). It should be noted that apart from French and Czech tanks, the Germans captured a number of others in the course of action, and re-modelled them: the Russian T.34 became the T.34.747, the American M.4 became the M4.748, and the British Matilda became the Mk.II.748.

Great Britain

Beginning from standard models, it can be interesting to build the special vehicles that were used at the time of the 1944 Normandy landings. A number of strange-looking machines were built, based on the Sherman—the Crab, the Scorpion, the Lobster, and the Lulu. These conversions can be done with the help of plastic sections, small chains and recovery materials. The Valentine and Churchill tanks underwent various modifications in the course of production, some of them external: modifications for river-crossing, flame-throwing etc. Reference to works on the history of armour will show the varia-

tions in cannon and equipment that appeared during the war. These various conversions are easy, as is the substitution of a 3-inch gun on the Matilda.

Italy

The 13/40 medium tank, available in the shops, can be used for conversions into the prototype Ansaldo L.3, or the 1939 M.II, the platform and the track assemblies remaining as they are: the changes are in the superstructure. Modification can be extended, to produce the observation tank, or even the most complicated version, the 15/42 with 47mm cannon to replace the 37mm.

Two details of the Jagdpanzer, the Wehrmacht's self-propelled gun or howitzer. This 1/35 Tamyia model is particularly well-made and easy to construct.

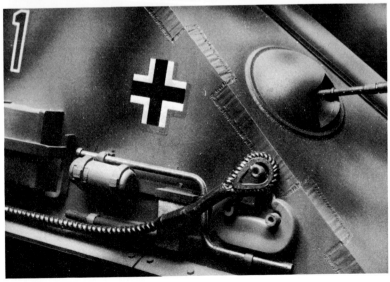

Suspension detail of the Sherman M.4 tank, Tamyia large-scale. Faultless!

Japan

There are not many models available on the market. Using the Shinhoto Chiha (type 97 medium tank) as the basic platform, the best one can do is to convert the turret to make the 75mm cannon model (type 3 Chin-Nu), which was equipped with a French Schneider gun. The Marder III turret can be used for this conversion.

Sweden

In 1938 the Czech TNH.SV. Skoda tank was ordered by the Swedish army. Delivery turned out to be impossible, but Scania Vabis acquired the licence. Using the PzKFw I (German) and a Marder (Czech-built for the Germans), you can make a model of this tank, of which only 238 were made. Using the PzKFw I bearing wheels, you can also build the STRV.M 38.

The U.S.A.

The number of tanks derived from the Sherman and the Lee are so numerous that there is no room to list them all here, but the variations among the models available mean that all sorts of permutations are possible, corresponding to modifications that actually occurred.

There are a number of things that can be added to the various Sherman M.4 tanks, including a number of rocket-launchers (the T34 E2, the T 72, the T 40 etc.). Anti-mine equipment used by the British army was also used on U.S. tanks. Sherman can

also be fitted with 'hedge-trimmers' (Normandy front, 1944). For those who like to build their own personal models from separate components, there are a certain number of American tanks which as far as we know are unobtainable in kit form: the heavy M6A2 (1940–3), the light M2 in its different versions, the light M3 (Tamyia do a version of the Stuart model, the platform and wheel and track assemblies of which can be used for a number of conversions), the light T.9, and the tanks in the T.4 series. These last ones, built between 1930 and 1937, served as models for the designs of the first Russian T.34s, and certain components of the T.34 can be used to make them, in particular the wheels of the 1943 model.

The U.S.S.R.

The various versions of the T.34, the KV I, the KV II and the SV.85 available in kit form can be used as platforms for the construction of the T.60–T.70 light tank series. The parts of the T.36 will also do—just about—for the building of the T.26. The wheel-train can be that of the KV II. The T.32, a medium tank that preceded the T.34, made in 1940, differs from it only in its more sharply-angles turret and shorter cannon. There are nine versions of the T.34 itself. The T.43 was a development from it. Starting from a model of the KVIC which is available, the very similar IB can be built, as can the streamlined IS version (S for Skorostnoy, which means high-speed). The KV.85 is essentially a KV.I platform with a modified, longer turret. One could also attempt the construction of the famous Joseph Stalin IS.85.

Materials for Conversion of Tanks

The materials we have discussed for conversion jobs on cars are also suitable for military vehicles. However, moulding is never a good idea. Plastic filler, better known as Body Putty, is preferred: this is a sort of plastic cement which can be used to change a component's shape in order to modify a turret, for example, or a cowling. Body Putty should not be over-used, but it is especially useful for made-to-measure parts. It should be worked on when in position.

Examples of camouflage in the field

Summer camouflage

Use of foam and flocking to make camouflage, the net made from a hairnet.

Twigs etc. can be used too

Using bits of lichen to get the effect of fresh greenery

Camouflage net

Winter camouflage

Mixture of light and dark colours from base to turret of the tank: white, green, brown

On certain tanks, and especially on self-propelled guns like the Elefant and the Jagdpanzer with poor visibility, the Germans used an anti-magnetic protective coating called 'zimmerit'. This was intended to inhibit the planting of mines by partisans, commandos and anti-tank units. This coating can be rendered very well in Body Putty, which is worked with the point of a tool.

Military Vehicle Camouflage

In this section we shall discuss both the details of how to put camouflage on scale-models, and the techniques worked out by the various military authorities between 1939 and 1950. The traditional kind of camouflage was more or less abandoned and then taken up again during the allied occupation of Germany and within NATO. In the case of nuclear warfare, camouflage presents problems when it comes to radiation protection.

Camouflage 1939–40

French army armoured vehicles were painted beige-khaki, the tanks being given a basic camouflage of brown, beige, and olive-green. A look at contemporary photographs shows that there was not one but a number of kinds of camouflage. B and D tanks were painted with a jigsaw-puzzle patterned camouflage that was basically beige and green. On the Hs (Hotchkiss) and the AMCs, the outlines of the camouflage were picked out in brown. British army tanks had a similar kind of camouflage, with beige and brown being used on the larger areas. Thanks to German air supremacy between 1939 and 1942, their armour at that time had no camouflage at all. They used grey paint, and sometimes added foliage. Camouflage is painted or sprayed onto armoured vehicles, and the same techniques apply to scale-models. The air-brush can give very good results if the body has been thoroughly prepared. A good practice is to use cut-out masks so the paint will not run outside the desired area. Maskol can also be used on the areas not to be painted; it can be removed afterwards with a pair of eyebrow tweezers. A kit generally includes instructions on camouflaging, and the paints to be used. As a general rule, use

the matt shades that they recommend— but use between 10 and 30 per cent of thinner to increase the washed-out appearance. Real-life tanks never had bright colours.

Camouflage 1940–5

Camouflage in the different armies varied with military requirements and the weather. So there was winter camouflage, desert camouflage, and so on. The manufacturers make recommendations with their kits, but corrections are always necessary, and the model must be suited to the scene.

When on operations, armoured vehicles and tanks were camouflaged with, as well as paint, foliage and branches, which were changed daily. They were not just dumped on, but fastened. For this, extra-fine metal wire can be strung along the sides of your models to hold foliage etc. Sprigs of briar can be used for the latter as they have a suitably twisted effect.

Camouflage nets can be made from fine netting dipped into a thinned mixture of brown and green. Afterwards it should be stretched out to dry flat. When dry, paint certain parts again to make the colours a bit more vivid, then apply a few drops of glue to the netting and sprinkle with brown and green flocking. The netting is now ready for use.

You can buy special transfers to be used on tanks. These are often more suitable than those supplied with the kits. The ESCI and Italerei ranges satisfy just about every need.

Ready-made Components for Building Dioramas

These are basic components for military scenes, available in 1/72, 1/43, 1/48 and 1/32, relief-moulded, measuring about 40 by 20cm. They can be used for trenches, shell-holed roads, artillery positions and breastworks, operational landing strips, supply points, blockhouses, landing beaches etc.

Smaller models can be equally well used in little tableaux. Standard dimensions are 26 by 11cm. There are bunkers, trenches, bridges, barriers etc. While Airfix produce ready-to-paint forts—Fort Apache, a Middle Ages castle, Waterloo, a Roman

Following page: Some small-scale (1/72) models. ESCI, experts on this scale, offer a large choice of vehicles and armour.
Above: A scout car.
Below: A Hanomag tracked armoured car and an artillery towing vehicle.

fort, etc., Armtec make scenery accessories at 1/76 (tools, weapons, spare parts).

Reference works available in libraries which are useful for conversions:

Bellona Publications (Great Britain).
'Tanks and Combat Records' (Aberdeen Proving Ground, Maryland, 1944).
'Handbook on German Military Forces' (War Department, Washington, 1945).

'Illustrated Record of German Equipment' (War Office, London, 1947).
Milson: 'Russian Tanks (1900–70)' (London and Harrisburg, 1970).
'Profils AFV': English language edition, with descriptions by model of British and German armour.
See also: The Royal Armoured Tanks Corps Museum, Bovington, Dorset, Great Britain.

Constructing and Displaying other Military Vehicles

Armies have other vehicles besides tanks. These days you can buy different kinds of trucks, staff cars, self-propelled guns and half-tracks in various scales—1/25, 1/32, 1/43, 1/48, 1/72 and 1/76. In these categories, the vehicles are generally British and American. Reconnaissance vehicles are on the whole well represented, particularly those in service with the German and American forces. Military trucks, on the other hand, are not so common. It is amazing that there are no models of the various GMC trucks which did such wonders for so long. Apart from the Opel Blitz, Germany is poorly represented, considering how many vehicles were made by Daimler-Benz, Krupp, Krauss Maffei, and Hanomag. The virtually international Fords are also missing from the catalogues.

Generally, when a tableau is being set up, vehicles other than tanks play a secondary role. Collections are of course enhanced by small-calibre artillery pieces and anti-aircraft guns, which are available in profusion. Nevertheless, there are still large gaps that remain to be filled.

Basic Colours for Military Vehicles

France: buff and khaki (1940).
U.S.A.: olive drab 613 brown and army X-24087, olive drab no. 41 and zira chromate.
Germany: Panzergrau (1939–43), 04 Gelb (official colour as from 1943).

Constructing and Displaying Aeroplanes

There is a multitude of ready-to-construct plastic scale-model aeroplane kits, on a host of different scales. The international brands are generally on the usual scales: 1/32, 1/43, 1/48, 1/55 and 1/72. There are also scales that vary somewhat, making it difficult to assemble a uniform collection—scales like 1/54, 1/55, 1/60, 1/63. Larger machines are available in scales varying between 1/80 and 1/100. Yet out of all this apparent chaos, it is still possible to create a reasonably consistent collection, as the choice is so very wide. In fact it would take 150 pages of catalogue to list all the models!

Assembly and Modification

All the techniques for assembly, glueing and painting already discussed apply equally to aeroplanes. It is particularly important to make sure that glueing lines disappear with the help of Body Putty.

Paint is applied in the ways we have covered already, with an airbrush, a spray gun, or a brush. The transfers supplied are often mediocre or at best not very accurate. Better to replace them with ABT, ESCI, or Italerei products; there are also micro-transfers—made by Micro Scale, specially designed for each type of plane.

There are two areas that deserve special attention: the cockpit, with its controls and instruments; and the engine, in so far as it will be seen (as with a jet, or a radial engine). After painting, planes should be finished in matt colour.

Conversion of standard kits into individual models, or as part of special series, can be done as follows:

Fuselage: Polystyrene can stand grinding, sawing and trimming. Very fine delicate work may not always be successful. Since this is so, always use jeweller's saws and files with polystyrene. To alter the volume of a component, there are three possible procedures. Fine sheets of balsa-wood or cartridge paper can be made to look like authentic plates, and are

Right-hand page, top: The ME 262, first operational combat jet (1944). A sombre look, representative of the times! Below: A Focke-Wulf 109 on the ground. Tableau includes ground staff.

Double page spread following: Left-hand page: Some models of galleons, carvels and other high-decked ships date from the 17th and 18th centuries. Right-hand page: Above: Prow detail from the 'Soleil Royal'. Below: The school-ship 'Pamir'.

Details of interior of a Mustang P.51

Facing page 97: What used to be called 'twin-tails': the Lightning P.38 (several makes including Monogram and Revell). The model shown here is exceptionally detailed; note especially the undercarriage. In real life, Second World War aircraft were basically of two kinds—those attacked without fear of counterattack were camouflaged; those that were part of formations and could be attacked, like this bomber, had a uniform colour. U.S. twin-engined aircraft were used as strike aircraft rather than long action raid bombers. Aircraft which acted independently, like the P.38, were more liberally camouflaged.

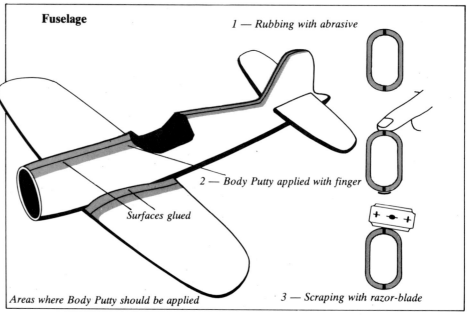

Fuselage

1 — Rubbing with abrasive

2 — Body Putty applied with finger

Surfaces glued

Areas where Body Putty should be applied

3 — Scraping with razor-blade

especially good for older planes. Thin pieces of plastic can also be stuck on to enlarge a fuselage. All seams should be concealed with Body Putty and smoothed over. Final shaping should always be done with the fingers, which are more sensitive than any tool. Finally, rub with a rag or with a paper handkerchief dipped in thinner. Final polishing will remove the last traces.

Wings: On older aeroplanes, certain details can be brought out. The wing-struts of a biplane can be particularly realistic. They can be made with extra-fine copper or steel wire. We do not recommend nylon thread, despite its elasticity, because it may break the wings on account of its tension. Struts can also be made with 0.2mm diameter stiff metal wire cut to the right length. For this, little depressions must be made in the wings to position the struts. A drop of varnish will suffice to hold them in place.

Wood, cartridge paper or plastic may be used for home-made parts. Copper or brass wire can be used for ducts, tie-beams and cross-rods—while flexible piping or wiring can be made of model railway electric wire. This comes in various colours, and the metal wire should be drawn out (and kept). The sheathing that is left is sufficiently flexible to be used, for example, on the engine or the undercarriage.

Certain models of contemporary aircraft or prototypes should not be painted. They should simply be covered with very flexible sheets of plastic metal. This is an excellent substitute for the old-fashioned 'silver paper' on chocolates.

Camouflage, Markings, Paintwork

Specialist magazines carry a lot of articles on the accurate painting and camouflaging of planes of all nationalities. In fact, when you buy a model in a shop, the instructions with the kit will be good for only one model, or two at best. Those who really have the collecting bug often find shop-bought products inaccurate or incomplete. The famous Spitfire, for example, which comes in every scale from 1/72 to 1/24, can be put together in about twenty different ways. There are detailed instructions, complete with colour illustrations, to help.

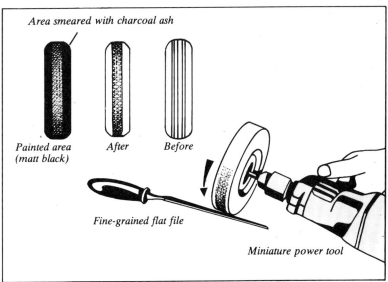

Area smeared with charcoal ash

Painted area (matt black) After Before

Fine-grained flat file

Miniature power tool

Above: A model of the celebrated American F 16.

Page 97:

Top: Plane made for the Chinese army (Warhawk P.40 and Mustang P.51 were the main ones).

Middle picture: Its Japanese rival. From 1942–4 the Jap Zero Kawasaki and Saiun Part were the principal adversaries of the U.S. models.

Below: U.S. first generation seaplane, 1940–5.

Conversion Kits

Most come on a scale of 1/72 (from Lindberg, Hasegawa, Airfix and Revell). With a kit, between two and four models in a set can be converted. To get the most from these conversion kits, you must study the available literature on each type of aircraft beforehand.

Displaying Aeroplanes

For the smaller scales (1/63, 1/72 and 1/83), there are various scene-setting accessories: storage tanks, tractors, people, shelters and so on (made by Airfix, Preiser etc.), which help to create little tableaux and dioramas. In 1974 Monogram published a simple document 'Tips on Building Dioramas' which explained in four pages how to display a basic model, a twin-engined Lightning undergoing repair during the War in the Pacific. Generally, the aeroplane or aeroplanes will be shown on the ground, on the runways, or outside their hangars. Another way, which takes up a lot of room, involves setting up an air-show or a club meeting.

Civil aviation and seaplane enthusiasts are less well catered for. However, they have greater scope for scene-setting: seaports, countryside, crowds, airline personnel etc., all available in different scales (Wiking, Preiser and Airfix).

Bomber cockpit details (Halifax)

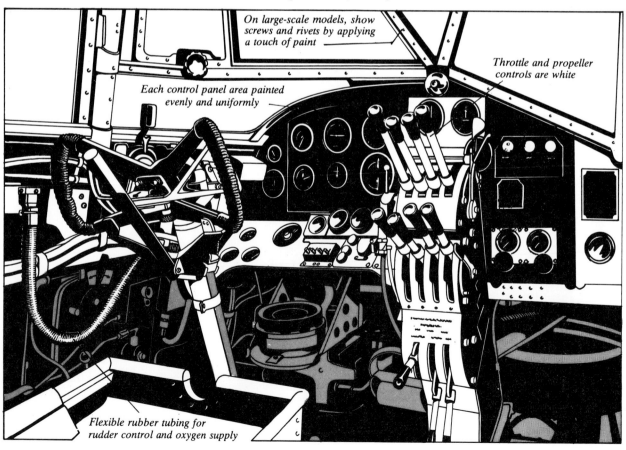

On large-scale models, show screws and rivets by applying a touch of paint

Throttle and propeller controls are white

Each control panel area painted evenly and uniformly

Flexible rubber tubing for rudder control and oxygen supply

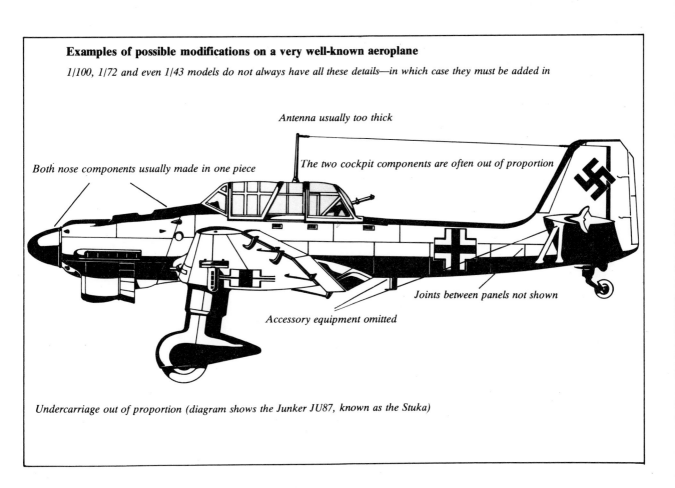

Examples of possible modifications on a very well-known aeroplane

1/100, 1/72 and even 1/43 models do not always have all these details—in which case they must be added in

Antenna usually too thick

Both nose components usually made in one piece

The two cockpit components are often out of proportion

Accessory equipment omitted

Joints between panels not shown

Undercarriage out of proportion (diagram shows the Junker JU87, known as the Stuka)

Constructing and Displaying Trains

In this area, the quality-minded scale-model enthusiast may find himself somewhat frustrated. The most common models are in the HO and N scales, which bear no relation to other areas of model making. However, some companies make 1/43 model trains, which allows other models to be brought in—people, vehicles etc. At present the Italian firm Rivarossi is producing locomotives of the American Far West, and a number of modern trains, both rolling-stock and engines—all on this scale.

Made of plastic, these models all come as construction kits, just like tanks and ships. However, certain metal components are made of bronze, as is the entire wheel assembly. It is simply a pity that there are

not more models of this kind. We feel sure there are many model enthusiasts who would rather have motor cars and locomotives at 1/43 than military hardware. On the larger scale, known as the I scale, L.G.B. and Pola make ready-made scenery and buildings. They do not involve much work and cannot easily be modified, but if nothing else they can be used as scenery for models on the same scale.

Conversions
In the case of large-scale railway models, there is little room for improvement—only modification and adaptation. With smaller scales, many accessories and pieces of scenery intended for 1/87 models can be used with 1/72. Level-crossing keeper huts, signals and other accessories are equally good for the two scales.

As for genuine conversions, all the techniques suggested for other kinds of model apply to railways. Carriages and locomotives can be converted and aged in the same ways as cars and lorries. All the practical suggestions for tanks apply to locomotives.

Constructing and Displaying Ships

1976 saw some well-orchestrated publicity campaigns designed to encourage the construction of model ships and boats. Obviously they are on a smaller scale than the models we have covered so far, for reasons of space. 1/700 models do not have very fine detail. On the other hand, there are some very handsome models in plastic and wood at scales ranging from 1/60 to 1/200. Some makes, like Monogram, spurn scale altogether and make all their models 43cm long. The largest model ship manufacturers are Heller, Aurora, Airfix, Hasegawa, Monogram and Tamyia.

Assembly and Modification
As far as the hull and basic superstructure goes, there is really nothing to add to what has already been said for other models. When it comes to detail, however, boats have certain peculiar characteristics. A drawing is provided showing the different parts of a ship, so that the beginner can find his way among the masts and sails to be assembled.

One main problem is the rigging on old ships. The main shrouds are made of plastic-covered wire. Before fixing, scrape the plastic to uncover the bare wire. This is

Cruel dilemma of scale and period. Which is better—a single handsome piece, or a more simple collection on a smaller scale? The choice is yours.

then glued on and held in place. Each rope is then stretched from the base point to the mast, and fixed with a drop of either glue or varnish. Tautening should be done before drying, using two alligator clips. Kit manufacturers usually keep quiet about the problems of assembling the masts and yards. Whether the mast is wooden or plastic, upward assembly of the three main components is always difficult, especially with the main mast.

On a real ship, the different pieces of a mast are lined up with each other and held securely by pieces of timberwork. This will not do for a model, so the timbers are replaced by fine nylon thread. The two parts to be joined are varnished. The thread is then coiled securely and, most important, in a regular spiral round both pieces, with a constant tension being maintained.

The numerous pulleys used on old-fashioned sailing ships can be made out of lead fishing weights or children's beads. Whichever is used, a coat of acrylic paint makes them look more realistic.

On many models, the hatchway grills

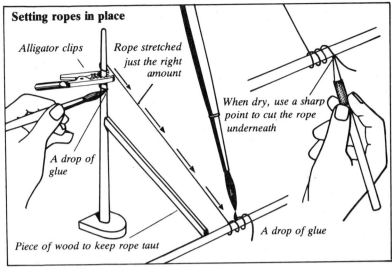

Setting ropes in place

Alligator clips

Rope stretched just the right amount

A drop of glue

Piece of wood to keep rope taut

When dry, use a sharp point to cut the rope underneath

A drop of glue

can be made out of mosquito or meat-safe netting. Ships are painted in the same way as other models, most of the paint used being matt. On present-day ships, only the porthole surrounds, certain hoisting equipment and hatches should have a shiny finish. It is wrong to lacquer a whole ship. The hull can be weathered as necessary, and dealt with like an aeroplane fuselage.

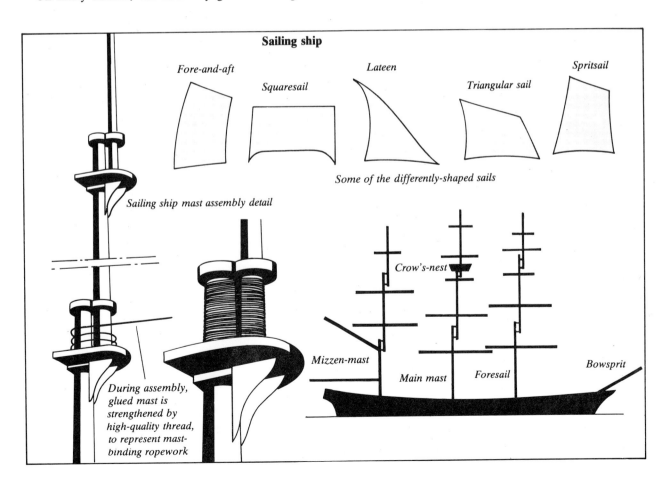

Sailing ship

Fore-and-aft

Squaresail

Lateen

Triangular sail

Spritsail

Some of the differently-shaped sails

Sailing ship mast assembly detail

During assembly, glued mast is strengthened by high-quality thread, to represent mast-binding ropework

Crow's-nest

Mizzen-mast

Main mast

Foresail

Bowsprit

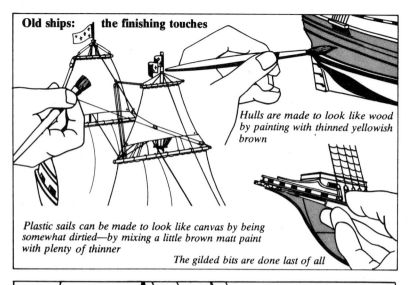

Old ships: the finishing touches

Hulls are made to look like wood by painting with thinned yellowish brown

Plastic sails can be made to look like canvas by being somewhat dirtied—by mixing a little brown matt paint with plenty of thinner

The gilded bits are done last of all

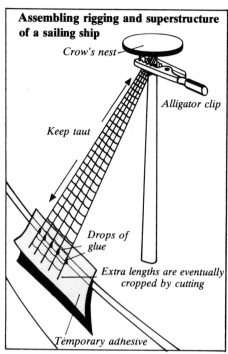

Assembling rigging and superstructure of a sailing ship

Crow's nest

Alligator clip

Keep taut

Drops of glue

Extra lengths are eventually cropped by cutting

Temporary adhesive

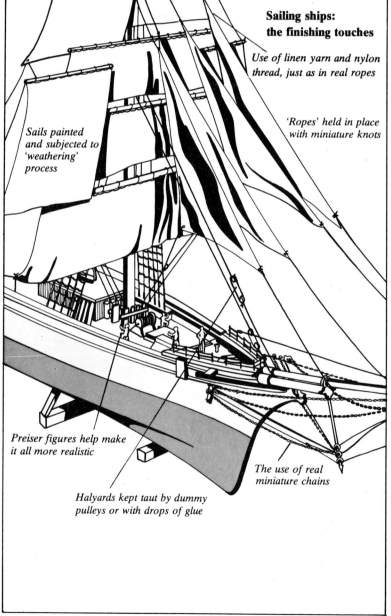

Sailing ships: the finishing touches

Use of linen yarn and nylon thread, just as in real ropes

'Ropes' held in place with miniature knots

Sails painted and subjected to 'weathering' process

Preiser figures help make it all more realistic

The use of real miniature chains

Halyards kept taut by dummy pulleys or with drops of glue

Attaching the various ropes and stays to the masts is always done last. Apply a drop of varnish to the lower point, extend the rope to the higher point, and fix it there with another drop.

All the techniques of ageing and weathering, rust, wear and tear etc. that we have already discussed apply to ships. The painting of plastic sails often presents problems. After a bit of practice, it is better to replace the original plastic ones with cloth, painted first on a flat surface before being mounted. The first coat should be half white and half cream, with 60 per cent thinner. The sail can then be mounted and creases and weathering drawn in in grey.

Sources of Information

Not everyone has access to the necessary reference works to learn all the details of the rigging, the sails, the cargo capacities, and the armaments of sailing ships, but visits to antique dealers and secondhand bookshops will yield very accurate old prints and models of sailing ships. Very often copperplate engravings—these reproductions have a two-fold interest: they can be used as background scenery for a model, and as a source of information for conversion purposes. Another very good source is the English Bellona series of publications.

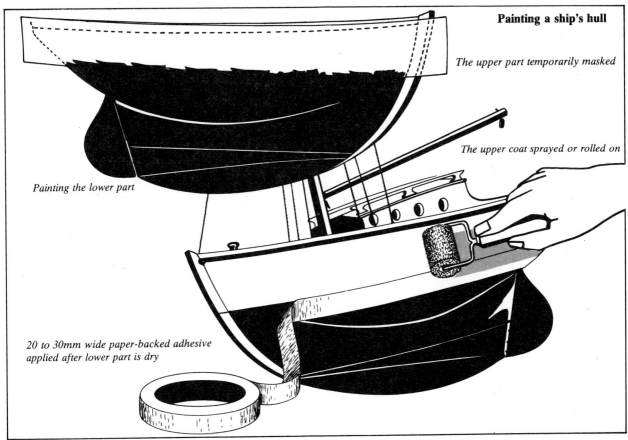

Painting a ship's hull

The upper part temporarily masked

The upper coat sprayed or rolled on

Painting the lower part

20 to 30mm wide paper-backed adhesive applied after lower part is dry

Scenery, Decoration and Enhancement of Models

The principles of scenery and settings do not change, whether the models are 1/72, 1/32 or 1/25.

Background Scenery

The display case, whether ready-made or in construction kit form, will eventually house a diorama—that is, scenery incorporating false perspective to resemble the horizon; or it would be a simple setting—in other words, a scale-model and its environment with facade, depth and height all on a constant scale.

In a diorama, only the foreground is to scale, and then the scenery gets smaller and smaller. The diorama has a foreground, sometimes kept to the simplest possible, a main area, a secondary area, and background scenery. The most difficult part is linking these different areas while maintaining continuity. Basically, a diorama is rather like a stage set, with similar conventions: the foreground quite flat (painted), the main area given maximum space, and the background painted in perspective. The foreground could consist of branches of a tree, the piers and arch of a bridge, or other detail which makes the scenery look normal when seen in a rectangle. When the eye passes around the horizon, it is as though you are looking in a curve. So the background of the diorama must be somewhat curved, at the edges if nowhere else.

For the background horizon line to appear horizontal, it must in fact go up at each end of the diorama. If the display case will be looked at slightly from below, this horizon line must not be placed too low. The base (i.e. the ground) must be tilted at an angle of about 5 per cent. From every point of view, there is room for numerous practical observations between the initial drawing on a piece of paper and the final finished model. In particular, it is useful to operate in the same way as if you were looking at a television screen (centre-on, of course).

Optical illusion also enhances the appearance of the models themselves. Anything in the foreground (or in front of it) must be precisely coloured and richly shaded. Colours in the secondary area or in the background will be far more fluid or thinned.

Apart from what is painted on cardboard or wood, background scenery also can have figures and accessories on a much smaller-scale than that of the foreground. A street in perspective, for example, might have in the foreground a 1/25 model, then 1/43 models, and in the background some 1/72 or 1/100 models. Here is the succession of scales that can be used in one or more settings: 1/25, 1/35, 1/43, 1/72, 1/76, 1/83 and 1/100. (These are all 'commercial' scales). Whatever the models used in the background, they should always be placed diagonally, facing right or left—but never perpendicular to the front. It is best to place them in the direction of a vanishing-trace leading to the vanishing-point. Ideally, scenery runs from the secondary area to the background, first three dimensional, and then continuing as painted scenery: the front of a building, the surface of water, a road, a hedge, or a line of trees. Care must be taken that the vanishing-trace causes no visual break with the areas further forward. An eye should always be kept on the inclination of the ground level (see diagram).

How to go about it?

Take a sheet or two of drawing paper and sketch your scenery. Mark where the buildings, mountains and fields will go, then set the drawing at the back of the display case. Then, with a little imagina-tion, you can envisage what the country-side will finally look like. Make any necessary changes, and then remove the paper. Cut out each separate area, and then use water-colours or poster paints to paint it on the selected material—wood, cardboard or plastic. The simple act of leaving a two or three millimetre gap between each component of the back-ground scenery will further increase the sensation of perspective and relief.

Putting the Scenery in Place

Once the proportions have been worked out, how is the scenery actually made? First volumes and colours must be balanced.

Sorting out the Volumes

Look first at the foreground and pre-fore-ground: these will be in the middle. In general, figures of people and things in the central area will be made from shop-bought models, whether modified or not. They must be made with special care and attention. Items of scenery in the middle background are made to size, using raw

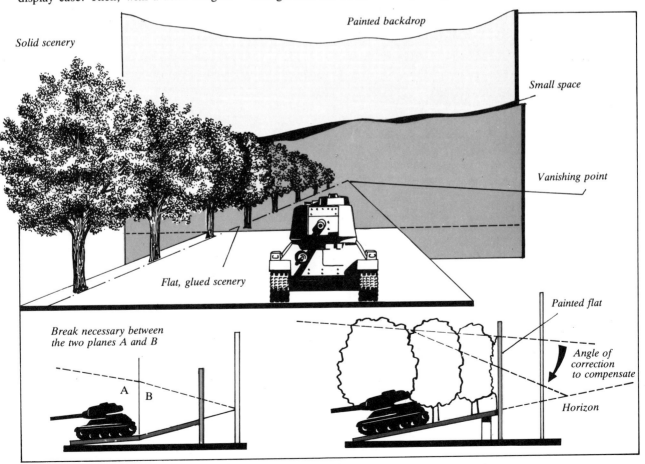

Solid scenery

Painted backdrop

Small space

Vanishing point

Flat, glued scenery

Painted flat

Break necessary between the two planes A and B

A | B

Angle of correction to compensate

Horizon

materials. Some items can be constructed using parts of models. If possible, this area should contain a flat vertical surface big enough to get the diorama effect. In the background, scenery can have less depth, or even none at all.

The Effect of Colours

Every setting must have a dominant colour: green for a wooded clearing, light grey in a street, blue-green for the seaside. Since, when it is painted, everything must be the correct colour, this effect of dominant colour must be got through the lighting or in the shading of the background.

The Illusion of Mass

Certain solid objects appear more massive than others through the 'redundancy' effect—a lighter shade showing up more prominently on a darker background. When making scenery, always bear in mind the tricks used for traditional theatrical scenery. 40 to 50 per cent of the objects must be in relief—anything medium-sized, ground surfaces, steps, columns and trees, telegraph poles and electric cables, shrubs and bushes, water, or people. While most flat surfaces can be satisfactorily done with tricks of perspective.

The Effects of Artificial Relief

It might be thought that the systematic use of in-the-round relief would be ideal for dioramas and models—it is not. Of course, your boat, your car or your plane will obviously be constructed entirely in the round. Most of the scenery around it can be in genuine relief too. However, certain parts can be made flat, using the illusion of perspective, a bit like stage scenery. This technique includes building facades and the 'backcloths' (the end of a room, or countryside etc.). However, you hesitate, because you are not very good at painting. Here is a simple way of getting dramatic perspective effects. On a piece of cartridge paper or Bristol-board, draw the main area and cut it out. In the secondary area, on another sheet, draw the doors and windows, getting smaller as they go back. Put both sheets together and shine a light along them horizontally. Mark the darkest areas of shadow with a pencil. These areas will be painted light grey. Then light the

sheet normally. See where the shadows appear and shade them in gently. This 'bas-relief' surface can then have relief accessories added—an electric sign, a balcony, timbers etc. but, of course, they must be taken into account when painting in shadows afterwards. Sometimes a simple wooden cut-out, a tube or a dowel to represent a moulded cornice, can be enough to bring out the relief, and to make the scenery exceptionally lifelike.

Town Scenes

Town scenes have two basic elements—streets and houses. On the HO scale, which goes with electric trains or small electric car tracks, there is seldom a problem. There are many construction kits available—but at 1/25, 1/35, 1/43 or 1/48 the problem is more complex because all buildings have to be constructed. The most popular material is thin plywood. The first thing to concentrate on is accuracy of detail. There will probably be two or three shop bought models, figures or accessories, that will be of more or less the right scale. So you must have documentation to ensure that the scenery is accurate. With 'Historex' figures this is very difficult, as a 19th century 'ambiance' must be created. Things are easier with a street scene set between 1900 and 1945. Be careful of historical errors—posters advertising products that did not exist at the time, or the inclusion of things, cars or scenery that were unknown at the time when your scene is supposed to have taken place.

We can say that the reproduction of life in a town is very difficult because it involves technical details and research. Here are various random details that apply to many towns before 1950:
—Some streets were cobbled.
—There was no fluorescent lighting. Street lights were either incandescent or gas, and they gave a rather weak light.
—Shopfronts were generally wooden and painted in dark colours, and they had different names from today. It goes without saying that snack-bars and mini-markets did not exist. Shopfront walls often had advertisements painted on them.

—There's no need to include television aerials, because they did not exist either.

For the craftsman-modeller, Morris columns, Wallace fountains and fire hydrants all represent little challenges which can become real masterpieces.

Making Things Flat and in Relief

Anyone who fancies himself as a painter can paint shopfronts and interiors simply in one dimension, flat, using an artist's techniques—false perspectives, heightened shading etc. Sometimes a sheet of drawing paper, painted and applied to a piece of plywood, itself painted, is enough to create relief and the illusion of volume. Use very matt paint at all times. Do not hesitate to use poster paints or modellers' acrylic paints. Avoid monotonous effects. After applying the undercoat, use an airbrush or spray-gun to apply two or three lighter shades. Only the fronts of cafés or the woodwork on shopfronts can be painted in bright colours. Street surfaces present the same problems as walls of houses: show cobbles by varying the colour with shades of grey, pink and blue. Finally, let us again stress that you must consult old magazines, books and postcards before undertaking a diorama of a town scene. We could say that the undertaking of a town scene should be the last in a series of creations. So we do not recommend it for the novice modeller, who will find country scenes easier.

Winter Scenes

Whether you are making a scene from the Battle of Stalingrad, a snow and ice car-rally, or the Battle of the Ardennes, there are certain special effects that must be incorporated:

Mud: Roads and pathways are a dirty mixture of melted snow and earth. This texture can be obtained by various means: mix sand or sawdust with burnt cork and dip the result into a dark grey poster paint. This gives a paste which is then set in place on a bed of glue, with a spatula. The relief effect is heightened by applying a light spray coat of dark brown or black followed by a light spray coat of artificial snow. You can find in the shops a special product for doing puddles.

Trees and bushes: Use brown, russet or grey lichen. The lower parts of bushes and tree-trunks should be dark grey, sprayed on if possible. Fir trees and evergreens amongst other trees should be painted a dark (French railway-carriage) green, as their colouring seems even denser in winter.

Snow: Two materials can be used—sheets of expanded polystyrene for the open stretches, and spray cans of Christmas decoration snow. The latter must always be applied very thinly. Matt spray paints can also be used.

Lighting: You can opt either for cloudy weather, or for a red sun. The principal light source of the scene should be low enough to make good long shadows. An opalized light bulb can be covered with a piece of black crêpe. Orange-red paint on a couple of patches will give the colour of a half-hidden sun. A 40-watt bulb, or a 20-watt night-light is sufficient to create the atmosphere. Auxiliary lighting is provided by a night-light masked with a piece of dark-coloured material. Between this source and the scene, you could also have a sheet of tracing paper or some dirty glass.

With a winter battle scene, place Christmas tree lights at the vital points, using only the red and the white bulbs. With the automatic oscillator, these give the flashing effect of explosions a long way off.

Lighting to Scale

The diorama, the stand, or the shelf where models are displayed, should have suitable lighting, which can be of various kinds. This lighting creates relief, but must not be used in place of light sources which can be made to scale. Lighting made to scale for models is generally things like the lights of electric trains (12–16 volts) or the lights inside radio equipment.

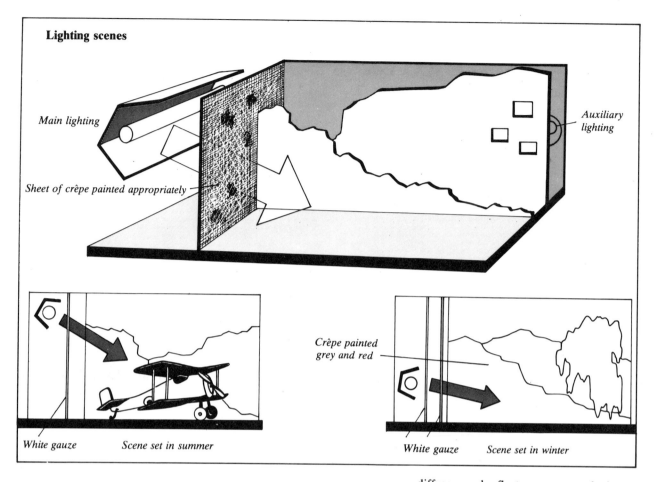

Lighting scenes

Main lighting

Auxiliary lighting

Sheet of crêpe painted appropriately

Crêpe painted grey and red

White gauze *Scene set in summer*

White gauze *Scene set in winter*

Lighting Buildings

Whatever the scale selected, it is adequate to use the light sources which are normally used for electric trains. They come as small sockets and the bulb is screwed into them. This kind of light can be placed inside buildings, in shop windows and in rooms. Varying degrees of shading, or the use of diffusers and reflectors, can vary the intensity of light appearing at each window. When model-makers hold exhibitions they link this kind of lighting to a rheostat. When the rheostat is wide open, all the lights in a building are on. As the rheostat is gradually closed, the building's lighting circuit gradually closes down until the only lights left are those that give a daylight effect. For anyone who is handy with electricity it is simple to put together, and gives dramatic effects.

Various manufacturers make street lamps, both standard and hanging types, intended for the lighting of N scale and HO scale electric train systems. These lamps can also be used for 1/72 and 1/43 scales, the sizes varying just as they do in real life. The L-G-B people, who make electric trains on the I scale, make lamps on the same scale. They are very suitable for scenery at 1/25 or 1/16.

Once the decorative trimmings have been removed, strings of Christmas tree lights can be used to illuminate advertisement hoardings, shop window decorations, or for indirect lighting.

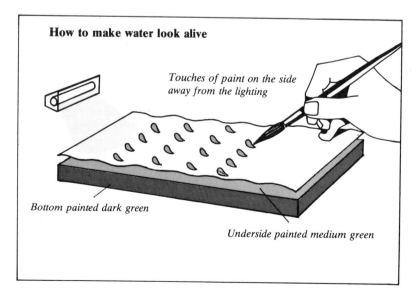

How to make water look alive

Touches of paint on the side away from the lighting

Bottom painted dark green

Underside painted medium green

Various Ways to Represent Water

A port, a landing scene, a river with fishermen, a viaduct—these all require water to be represented.

Water that is moving; a river: The classic material that has always been the professional modeller's favourite is opaque glass. Painted in grey-green shades, the wavy surface looks like the moving surface of a lake. It does well for 1/43, 1/72 and 1/100. For 1/16, 1/25 and 1/35, it looks no more than choppy. Be sure always to use any given colour on the same side of the waves. For example if you choose a grey-green, only use this shade on the right side. This gives an idea of where the sun is. Thus the painted part must face away from the lighting.

The effect of depth is made by painting the bottom of the piece of water a dark green, and the underside of the glass a medium green. The glass can be replaced by natural resin, but it is recommended for use on small surfaces.

A small stretch of calm water: The bottom should either be modelled out of plastic, or made from a piece of polystyrene etched with solvent. It is painted grey-green with poster paint. A few pieces of green and grey lichen will do for the vegetation in a pond. Over all this a piece of sea-green crêpe is placed, and on top of it a piece of either altuglass or transparent glass. The glass can be painted a thinned pure green on the underside, but this can be judged once it has all been put together. A product called Aqua-cote allows extremely realistic ponds, streams and rivers to be made very simply.

A waterfall or a mountain stream: The most difficult forms of water to make! The basic ingredient for the rushing water is crumpled tissue paper mixed with crumpled tracing paper, or it can be done with resin. The whole thing is very lightly sprayed a matt white. The surface behind the waterfall, or the bed of the mountain stream, is made out of a sheet of rhodoid with a few traces of green paint on it. To make foam, squirt some artificial snow at either the top or the bottom of the model. Rocks, stones and vegetation beside the water should be sprayed with varnish to give the effect of water and spray.

The Countryside, The Vegetable Kingdom

We shall deal with vegetation quite separately from any consideration of scale. Anywhere from the 1/72 used for model aeroplanes to 1/25, the materials and the same methods can be used with equal success. In this area, there is a vast choice of products, mainly aimed at model railway enthusiasts. Here we shall only give some indications of the basic principles of construction and choice of materials.

How are Hills and Relief Features made?
In a small-scale scene, say 1/83, a 30 or 40cm high dome can easily represent a mountain with tunnels for railways and roads going through it, but at 1/25 it will be no more than a large rock. In fact assembly procedures do not change at all. Start by making some shapes out of thin plywood. These shapes are braced, and they can then be cut with a jig-saw or small fret-saw. They are then fixed onto their support with wood glue. Sometimes additional corner-bracing is a good idea. The whole thing is then covered with thick kraft paper, stapled on. Cliffs and bluffs can be made very realistically with cork-oak bark (grey or grey-green in colour) placed upright, or with pine bark (red-brown). They are then placed on the slope itself. Liquid glue should then be applied to the paper still showing in the gaps. These are then filled with any suitable filler that can be spread with a knife.

Making a relief feature

Hessian stapled on

1 — Box

2 — Special hydrozell-type plaster spread with spatula

3 — Undercoating sprayed on, followed by application of glue

Pieces of cork-oak bark

Additional relief and joins done with modelling plaster

4 — Flocking sprinkled through a sieve

5 — Putting plants and trees in place

Minerals and moraines can be made with sand, pebbles, cork bark and cork-dust

For the larger surfaces, the following mixture should be prepared: one part vinyl paint, one part modelling plaster, and one part filler. This gives a mixture at once oleaginous and granulated, which can be applied with a knife or by hand (wear rubber gloves). Sand, gravel or sawdust can be added at will to this mixture, depending on the desired finish, but the mixture is very heavy. So cellulose paste, although certainly more expensive, is preferred as it is much lighter. In the case of really bulky hills and mountains (more than 1 or 1½ metres long), it is a good idea to reinforce the kraft paper backing with wire mesh, stapled in place. Reinforced thus, the scenery has no chance of collapsing.

Preparation of fillers: The surfacing used to represent earth is prepared in the following way: mix a little vinyl paint (brown or grey) in a receptacle of water so that the water becomes the colour of the ground, the mixture remaining fluid. Then sprinkle in fine modelling plaster and stir. After a few moments, a gritty, friable paste will result. Then add cellulose filler; this will give the mixture a certain mellowness, and will prevent crumbling later. It can be applied by hand or with a spatula, whichever you prefer. Before the mixture dries, you can set pieces of scenery in it, such as boulders and trees—but this is not always possible.

How are Minerals made?
We have made a basic framework and now we have to decorate it. Here again, consulting tourist guides, books and post-cards will give precise indications as to what a particular piece of countryside looks like. Colours, the way shadows lie, and the textures of things will be of help. To make minerals, you will use a conglomeration of natural substances and shop bought products. Sand, sawdust and gravel will always be useful. Chunks of porous stone like the ones used between railway sleepers, splintered shale and bits of mill-stone will make good boulders. The only trouble with these materials is that they make the model rather heavy—weight being number one enemy for models displayed in glass cases. Pieces of half-burned charcoal are equally realistic for darker-

coloured rocks like granite and slate, and are very light. Modelling shops sell all kinds of powdery materials in packets, including special coloured sawdust and granulated cork. These can be used for building embankments, roads, railway beds and so on. They come in any number of colours, can be stuck on with liquid glue, and set in position with a blotter or a roller. Sheets of broken-off chunks of cork (available from interior decorating shops or home-brewing suppliers) can be used to make rocks, ruins, or sections of walls made out of stone or natural blocks. They can very easily be painted with poster paints.

How is Vegetation made?

One of the easiest ways is by using natural vegetation—worm-eaten branches, twigs, heather foliage etc. Owing to its shape, heather is particularly satisfactory for making tree trunks. Stripped of its bark, it can be painted very dark brown, pinewood red or white, depending on how the bark should look on the scale-model. The paint can be sprayed on, or the heather can be dipped into a poster paint preparation. The leafy twigs of certain evergreen conifers with their fine needles can also be used, provided they are prepared before-hand: after cutting, the branch is given two or three coats of a plastifying spray or varnish, at twenty-four hour intervals. This mummifies it, and it can now be covered with glass wool fibres, powder, or synthetic green decoration according to the desired final look. It is then all painted dark green. It should be examined after drying for two or three days to see that there is no incompatibility between the plastifier and the paint.

Foliage of a number of different kinds can be applied to real twigs or branches—powder in packets, treated lichen, sawdust etc. Once the wood is painted, it is coated with a special aerosol glue. Then use a brush or miniature tweezers to apply the tiny pieces which will serve as foliage.

Unlike what you can collect yourself in the woods, Iceland moss has been treated so it will remain supple for a long time. It is sold in little bags, in separate or mixed colours. It is ideal for doing bushes and shrubbery, and can also be strung out along twigs to make the foliage of small trees. The colouring can be varied some-what by using an airbrush to project paint. Indeed, when you look at trees in real life, they are never one uniform colour. The airbrush means you can make them look autumnal by using red and golden tints.

How are Fields and Meadows made?

The easiest way is to use rolls of imitation ground which are glued or stapled onto the surface. They come in various shades of green, in rolls measuring 2 by 1.2 metres. Flocking can equally well be used for an embankment, a hillside, or a sloping area. Green flocking and glue can be bought at modellers' shops. Flowers and cultivated plants can be made from little pieces of foam, sold in packets. For HO scale-models, the German firm of Faller publishes an annual brochure entitled 'The Countryside for Model Railways'. This covers the basic principles of vegetative scenery—with, in particular, numerous details of how to make a hop-field or a vine-yard! We must also not forget Preiser, who make numerous HO (1/87) scale accessories to make the fields even more lifelike.

Applying flocking: Flocking is composed of green- or brown-coloured particles which, when used, give a relief effect to vegetable and mineral materials in the scenery. Flocking powders come in various sizes of grain. Flocking is used as follows: the surface to be covered receives a coat of special glue, either sprayed or brushed on. The flocking is spread out on a fine sieve or sifter. By scratching the inside, you make the flocking fall in a thin layer onto the surface to be decorated. Make sure no part is left uncovered. Do not be afraid of putting it on too thick. After drying, a quick run over the scenery with a vacuum cleaner will suffice to remove excess particles. The areas with flocking (the surface of an embankment, a road, the prairie etc.) should not end abruptly where the glue ends. The coloured effect is continued by a fusion of colours. For example, at the edge of an area with green flocking on a uniform beige background, there will be some touching-up with paint. This technique is essential when making mountainous scenery.

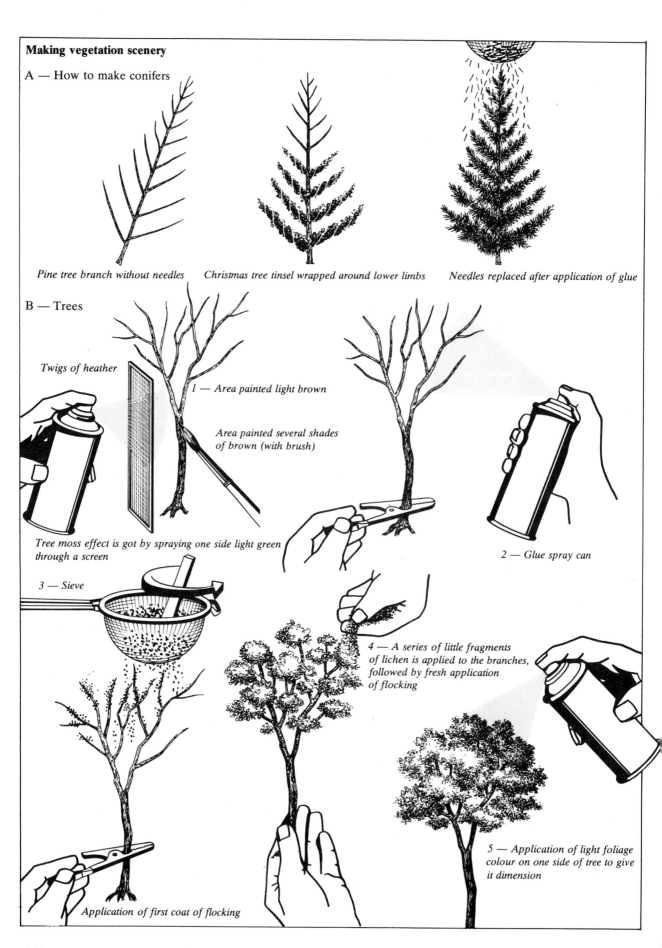

Making vegetation scenery

A — How to make conifers

Pine tree branch without needles

Christmas tree tinsel wrapped around lower limbs

Needles replaced after application of glue

B — Trees

Twigs of heather

1 — Area painted light brown

Area painted several shades of brown (with brush)

Tree moss effect is got by spraying one side light green through a screen

2 — Glue spray can

3 — Sieve

4 — A series of little fragments of lichen is applied to the branches, followed by fresh application of flocking

5 — Application of light foliage colour on one side of tree to give it dimension

Application of first coat of flocking

Scenery for Railway and Road Systems

Although model electric trains deserve a whole book to themselves, it is worthwhile studying the general subject of presenting railway systems in their environment. Bridges and viaducts, roads and stations present problems of positioning and accuracy, as well as of construction, that have more than one point in common with other scale-model scenery. We also include miniature car tracks (but not racing tracks) because, if they were more familiar, they could be more widely developed.

Stations and Railway Buildings

We shall leave on one side the layout and technical set-up involved with a model railway system. We are concerned with the HO scale (track width 16.5mm, scale 1/87) and the N scale (track width 9mm, scale 1/100), for these involve genuine 'all-round' model making. Rather than making an apparently complete railway system, it may be better to construct partial scenes. Thus on a wooden base measuring 1.5 by 0.8 metres you can make a goods depot or passenger station. A round table (1.2 metres across) can support a fine circular engine shed. The creative satisfaction will be just as great as with a diorama or any other model construction.

Practical Problems

On small scales, railway and roadside scenery has certain peculiarities. Far less emphasis is placed on accuracy of detail and relief than on the model itself, on the intensity of its colours, and on its technical fidelity.

Bridges and Viaducts

A bridge between two hills is most often built with prefabricated, shop bought components (embossed plastic sheets). If the bridge straddles a valley, these sheets will have to be fastened to a sloping area. The bridge could also have a road going across above a railway—what is known as an overpass. If the road is underneath, it is called an underpass. The piles can all be made out of balsa, which is easy to cut, and reinforced by small wooden sections. Next comes the facing of the retaining walls, the piers, and the embossed and glued cardboard arch. The plastic road surface and pile copings will be painted to make them look weathered. The effect of natural dirt is created by applying cigarette ash and powdered charcoal. Remaining weathering is done with beige and grey matt paint. The shape of a curve in a plastic component can be altered by using a small file to score the outer surface. For an HO scale electric train, the following dimensions are necessary to allow it to pass under a bridge: 37mm width, 50mm height—provided of course it goes under at right angles.

Building a metal viaduct is a work of art. It is simpler to use a shop bought ready-made model, and glue the pieces together. To make your own 'individualized' bridge, you can use construction kit parts together with sections made from raw materials, which can be easily cut with a jeweller's saw and shaped with a flat file. After assembly, all components must be repainted to make them look like real metal.

Hills, Cuts and Fills

Everything said about electric train and miniature car systems applies equally to other kinds of scenery on the various scales.

Relief features need supports, and these should always be made as slender as possible. Thus thin sections of plywood, easily cut with a jig-saw, can be glued into grooves of the same width, and reinforced with brackets. This structure is then the base for the relief material—wire gauze, metal or plastic netting, kraft paper, hessian etc.

The materials we have described in the foregoing pages are then placed on this support—earth, rocks, grass etc. The supports must be at once solid, and light, and they must certainly not be thought of as movable, except in part. Thus on the slope beside a track there will be a noticeable line, which will also correspond to the movable part of the relief. A sheet of plywood can be used to embed the structure,

Facing page 112: After-castle of the 'Soleil Royal', a Heller prestige model, scale 1/100, length 77cm, height 74cm.

How should figures be realistically presented?
Left-hand page,
above: Moroccan troops (Heller).
Below: U.S. unit of the 1950s. Every detail contributes to the authenticity.

which is fixed with large staples. Only then do you proceed to preliminary painting etc.

Interfacing material can also be used as a base, stiffened with wood glue. Scale-model specialists recommend yet another material—Faserit. Faserit is made of white flakes looking rather like some washing powders. Mixed with water, it forms an oleaginous paste which can be applied with a knife or a spatula. It is much lighter than plaster and can be applied to any foundation with a mesh of up to 2.5 or 3mm. It can then be painted with poster or vinyl paints, and sprinkled with flocking. Unlike plaster, this cellulose-base material goes soft again when remoistened, so that all sorts of alterations and improvements are possible after the initial shaping. Finally, one cannot overstress the point that this material is much lighter than plaster. Hydrozell is the brand-name of a product similar to Faserit, both of which are designed specifically for modelling. (See the section on know-how for the use of other materials which can be used in making relief features).

Making Railway Beds and Gravel Roads
Railway bed ballast comes in grey, brown or beige cork particles that can be glued. The principle is easy, but actually doing it can sometimes be tricky. When fixing any of these gravel-type surfaces, do not use glue that forms strands, as this prevents the cork particles from separating out and makes them stick together in lumps. Vinyl glue works better. For best results it is a good idea to prime the surface with a wooden roller; this will make adhesion more efficient.

Choosing a Position
While dioramas and small particular scenes can be displayed in glass cases, large model road and railway systems must be placed on a table or something similar. Once again, the limiting factor is the availability of space.

On a Frame or Panel
A wooden frame measuring one to two metres long and between a half and one metre wide can be made out of 25−30mm slats or laths, which are joined and glued together. The frame has corner supports. It is now ready to take the scenery and its base; this will be made out of chipboard or plywood between 10 and 20mm thick, according to surface.

With plywood, the following weight limits should not be exceeded: for a thickness of 8mm, 13-kilos between two support points 40cm apart; for 15mm thickness, 45-kilos between two points 50cm apart; and for 20mm thickness, up to 57-kilos between two points 60cm apart.

The ideal construction is one that is joined, glued, and finally screwed together. Nails should not be used as they tend to cause crookedness. When making a supporting frame, always allow for possible subsequent extensions of length and/or width, and for it to be moved; even if the frame is to remain stationary, equip it from the very beginning with handles or castors.

The classic and most simple kind of support for large items is trestles. They are also cheap. Ceiling suspension is acceptable, provided suitable eye-bolts are used (chandelier type). Hinged construction is complicated and, moreover, it means that the underside of the mounting board has to be decorated somehow, if only to hide the electric wires.

The Construction of Buildings

The quality of the buildings sets the tone of an entire scene. Buildings are most easily constructed on scales between 1/72 and 1/43. On smaller scales the details disappear, and on larger scales you need to be a real architect.

Building in Different Styles

Use books and postcards to get ideas of regional building styles. Then make a tracing, on drawing paper, that will serve as a basis. The building will be drawn on drawing paper and then cut out, the pieces standing against a supporting structure. For farm buildings and old-fashioned low-roofed farmers' houses, the support is made of light plywood or cardboard. For a mediaeval-type tall house, or a factory, the interior will contain a wooden supporting structure.

Walls

Apart from the central drawing paper design, cork, wood and painted heavy-duty cardboard can be used for extensions. So too can embossed sheets (scales 1/87 to 1/72).

Chimneys

It is best to cut these from a painted wooden lath or from cork blocks, depending on the style selected. Chimney pots and cowlings can be made from salvaged cotton reels.

Roofs

On large scales (1/35 and upwards), it is worthwhile making a real framework with wooden cross-pieces whose size will vary according to the scale. (See the glossary for what can be bought in the shops). Most illustrated dictionaries contain up-to-date plans of roofing frames. A kraft paper base is glued onto the frame, and tiles cut from cardboard are laid either in strips or as individual tiles.

Windows

Two materials can be used—cartridge paper or wood. Wood is more solid, but is more difficult to cut. The interior can be backed with rhodoid.

Architectural Details

Wood, cellulose putty and cardboard can be used to reproduce extremely realistic door frames, windows, facades etc.

How to build a house? Notwithstanding the numerous possible ways available in the shops, one is frequently obliged to construct buildings to measure. See pages 116–117 for how to go about this.

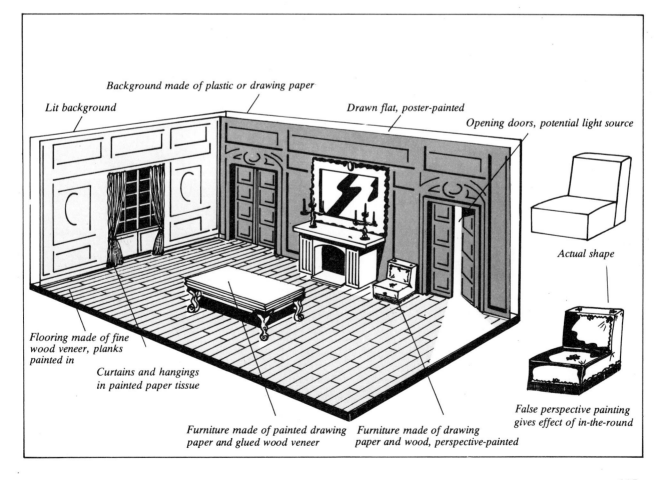

Background made of plastic or drawing paper

Lit background

Drawn flat, poster-painted

Opening doors, potential light source

Actual shape

Flooring made of fine wood veneer, planks painted in

Curtains and hangings in painted paper tissue

Furniture made of painted drawing paper and glued wood veneer

Furniture made of drawing paper and wood, perspective-painted

False perspective painting gives effect of in-the-round

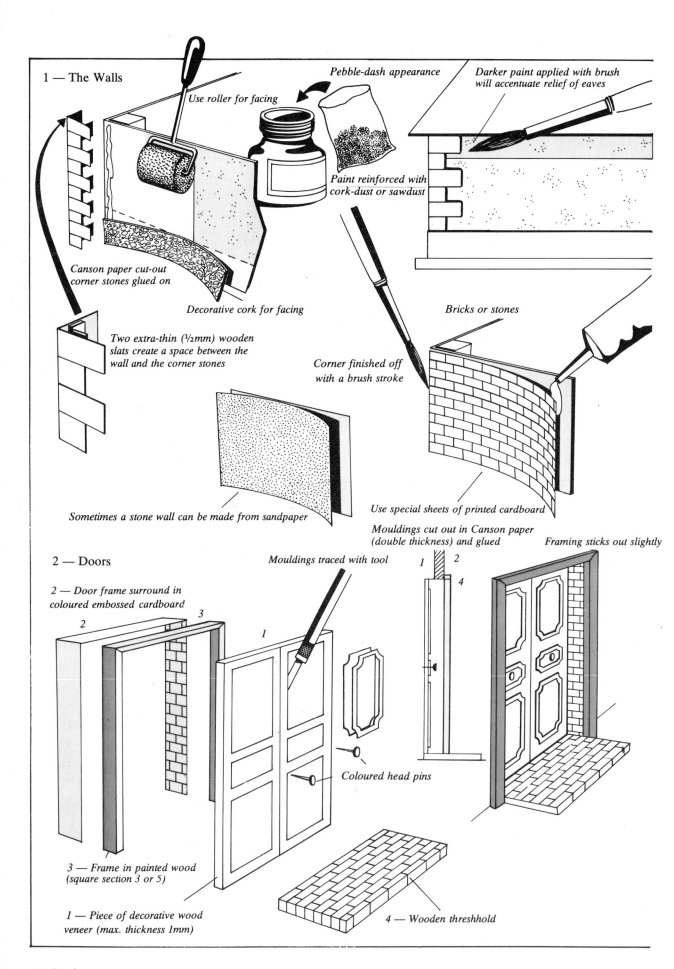

1 — The Walls

Use roller for facing

Pebble-dash appearance

Darker paint applied with brush will accentuate relief of eaves

Paint reinforced with cork-dust or sawdust

Canson paper cut-out corner stones glued on

Decorative cork for facing

Two extra-thin (½mm) wooden slats create a space between the wall and the corner stones

Corner finished off with a brush stroke

Bricks or stones

Sometimes a stone wall can be made from sandpaper

Use special sheets of printed cardboard

Mouldings cut out in Canson paper (double thickness) and glued

2 — Doors

Mouldings traced with tool

Framing sticks out slightly

2 — Door frame surround in coloured embossed cardboard

Coloured head pins

3 — Frame in painted wood (square section 3 or 5)

1 — Piece of decorative wood veneer (max. thickness 1mm)

4 — Wooden threshhold

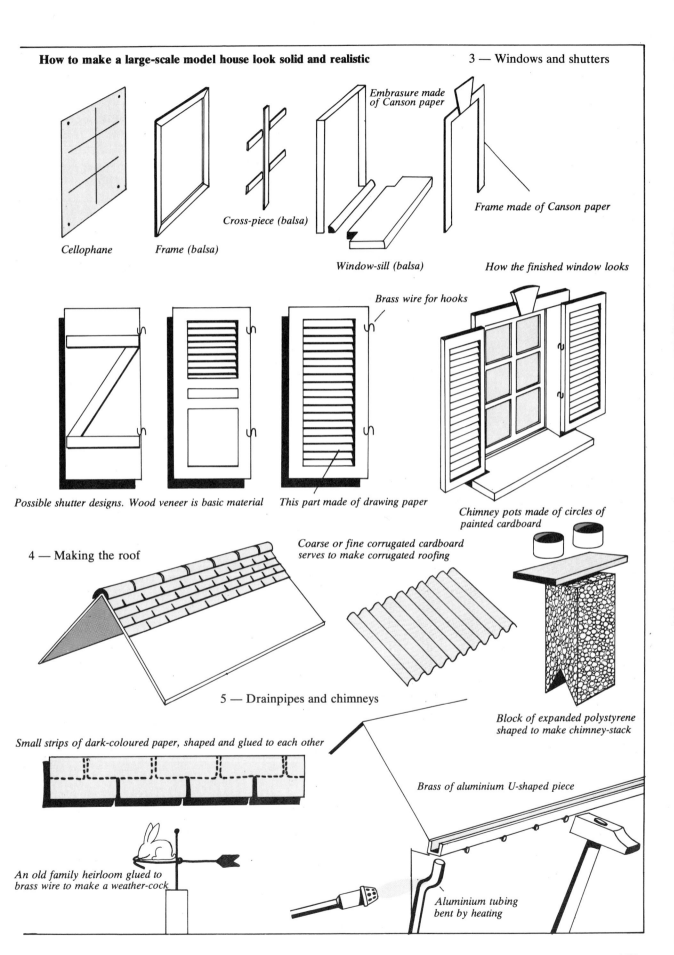

How to make a large-scale model house look solid and realistic

3 — Windows and shutters

Cellophane

Frame (balsa)

Cross-piece (balsa)

Embrasure made of Canson paper

Window-sill (balsa)

Frame made of Canson paper

How the finished window looks

Possible shutter designs. Wood veneer is basic material

Brass wire for hooks

This part made of drawing paper

Chimney pots made of circles of painted cardboard

4 — Making the roof

Coarse or fine corrugated cardboard serves to make corrugated roofing

Block of expanded polystyrene shaped to make chimney-stack

5 — Drainpipes and chimneys

Small strips of dark-coloured paper, shaped and glued to each other

Brass of aluminium U-shaped piece

An old family heirloom glued to brass wire to make a weather-cock

Aluminium tubing bent by heating

Interior Decoration

This hardly figures on scales of 1/100 to 1/43, where it is mass alone that counts, but from 1/25 to 1/8 interior decoration really comes into its own.

Lighting

Windows and other openings must be backlit in such a way that it looks as though the light is coming in from outside. The best source for outside lighting is a miniature fluorescent bulb of the bedside-light type. In some cases (the interior of a grotto, a pill-box, or a church, for example), an opening gives a single strong shaft of light. The directional light source must in that case be very well shielded.

Installation

In the chapter on figures, we outlined the general principles of producing scenery to go with them. Furniture is improved by being made out of wood. Real cloth or, even better, cloth-mesh should be used for hangings and wall decorations. Everything else can be put together from drawing paper, but once again, a number of small objects can be of assistance—press-studs or lengths cut from cardboard cylinders to make containers, pots or cans of food. Heller, Historex and other firms make genuine accessories to go with your own 'made-up' decor.

Generally speaking, if the tableau is to be viewed face-on, most elements of the decor can be made flat, and helped by false perspective. If, on the other hand, it will be viewed from three-quarters, everything must be made in three dimensions.

The Display and Protection of Models

The question of display is often dealt with too late. A model-maker's first model always ends up on a piece of furniture, but it's different when there are ten, fifteen or twenty models to find a place for. It is no longer a question of finding a place, but of displaying one's creations.

Glass Cabinets

New easy-to-assemble cabinets are displayed each year at the Do-it-Yourself Exhibition and in furniture galleries. Made out of aluminium or wood, and glass, they all have basically the same design: wooden boards are held in a box-shape on a supporting base by means of either hooks or braces. Sheets of glass are then slid into place. Some glass cases are totally enclosed. Glass show-cases of the kind used in museums are very expensive, but they are ideal for the display of a number of models.

The perfect display case is no more than 2 metres high and 60 to 70cm deep. It is a good idea to place a false cupboard or box underneath it, because one doesn't want to have to crouch to admire the models. If the models are to be seen from one side only, then the case should be backed up against a wall. Indeed this is essential with dioramas. A lockable cabinet is always desirable, so that children cannot get their hands in and start 'playing'.

Interior lighting of the cabinet can be provided with small 20-watt 'daylight' type fluorescent tubes. These work both for you and against you—but they cast a shadowless light. This enhances isolated models, and indeed the whole case. On the other hand, little tableaux and dioramas are enhanced by directional incandescent lighting—reflecting battens or a small 40-watt spotlight. Ideally the lighting switch will have two positions: full and directional.

Partial Display Cases and Bubbles

Elsewhere, (in the glossary at the end of

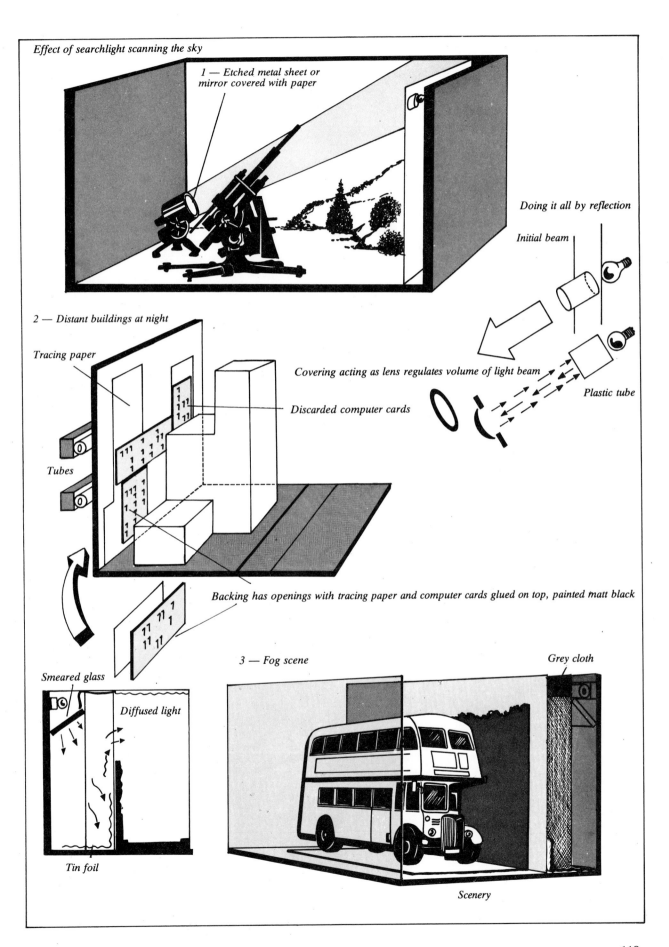

Effect of searchlight scanning the sky

1 — Etched metal sheet or mirror covered with paper

Doing it all by reflection

Initial beam

Covering acting as lens regulates volume of light beam

Plastic tube

2 — Distant buildings at night

Tracing paper

Discarded computer cards

Tubes

Backing has openings with tracing paper and computer cards glued on top, painted matt black

Smeared glass

Diffused light

Tin foil

3 — Fog scene

Grey cloth

Scenery

the book), we give the standard dimensions of plastic domes, or bubbles. They are widely used at exhibitions and for making closed-system gardens, and they are expensive—but they are ideal for showing off aeroplanes which are usually seen from all angles. They can be hung with piano wire or nylon thread, at various heights from the ground. Thus, on a one metre square floor surface, eight or ten bubbles could be strung up to the ceiling. These plastic shells come in small sizes for display of single small-scale models (1/100 or 1/83: people, cars) on a shelf or a piece of furniture.

Models can be given their own individual display cases, in glass or plastic. Another time-saving way of solving the problem is to buy a ready-made aquarium, put it on its side, and put the model in it. An individual display case can be glass or plexiglass.

Do-it-Yourself Display Cabinet

If you need to make a number of display cases to show off a collection, you must first make a rectangular piece of wood with two grooves set as far apart from each other as possible. Glass or plastic sheets will slide into these grooves, the bottoms of which have glue in them, two at a time. They are set exactly at right-angles and tied into position. The cabinet bottom can be a sheet of wood, the grooves made with a chisel (so do not use plywood). The four uprights are now in place. Last comes the lid. For certain scenes or historical models, the five transparent sides of the case are set off by little brass corner angles cut in a mitre-box. Old ships, or very large-scale models need well-made showcases.

Labelling

In a collection, each model must have a precise label, giving the date and how long it took to make, as well as a brief description (maximum three lines) of the real thing. While remaining readable, labels should be small. Scale-models almost always come with rather detailed documentation, and you can usually cut out a heading or an emblem to stick onto your own label. Transfers can be used to make really good labels.

Various kinds of Lighting

As we have seen, fluorescent lighting gives a shadowless light that covers the entire show-case or display shelf. The tube should always be 40 to 50cm above the models, with a 'diffusing' grill between. Highly directional spots of the kind used for reading at night are extremely useful for dioramas. The light is concentrated in a 3 to 4cm beam which carries accurately for 90 to 120cm. These spots, available from modern lighting shops, have the additional advantage of needing a simple clamp to mount them. The lighting can be horizontal, overhead, or oblique, depending on the degree of drama required in the scene. The combined effect of fluorescent tube lighting and directional spots does a great deal for dioramas, but beware: lighting can also show up any faults.

Special effects can be got with lights originally designed for use in an aquarium. They give a purplish-pink light which is perfect for dusk effects. Black lighting can be useful for making certain mechanical models stand out—engines, locomotives etc.—because it picks out shapes with very great precision.

Technical Glossary of Products and Raw Materials

Whatever the kind of model you want to make, you are faced sooner or later with using raw materials, metal or wood, that must be worked. When we speak of raw materials, we mean lengths of wood, laths, tubes and variously shaped sections sold in modellers' supply shops. Thirty or forty years ago, these were the model-maker's basic materials. In the chapter on know-how we had a look at other materials which could be useful.

Working from a scale-diagram, the model-maker used to make everything himself, often successfully. Today, modelling can and must be within the reach of everyone, and those who are not particularly skilful at working in wood or metal can make something without too many problems. This chapter aims to present a catalogue of everything that can be purchased, so that model-makers, both experts and beginners, can learn to recognize exactly what is available to them. These are the basic materials for all modelling jobs, whether you are converting or modifying an existing model or, like some true artists, creating it from raw materials.

Wood

As we see from the chapter on know-how, wood is the basis of certain types of boat and aeroplane, but its most common use is in the making of practically all kinds of scale-models. Easy to work and to smooth, wood is more rigid than cardboard and paper. Model-making shops sell various qualities of wood: rectangular or square-shaped pieces, and wood veneer. In do-it-yourself and decorating shops, wood veneer comes in rolls or sheets in the following finishes: oak, mahogany, teak and citron wood. Veneer is economical, but fragile and difficult to work; and it must be used only in sheets or facings which can be painted or varnished—for things like the facades of chalets, cabins, decks of ships, partitions, roofing etc.

Quality of Woods

Balsa: the model-maker's wood, the one that has been in use the longest. It was being used to make model aeroplanes in the 1930s and 1940s. Its most significant characteristic is its lightness (it weighs 0.21−0.25 grams per cubic centimetre). Being soft and porous it is difficult to paint, to shape, and to smooth, but despite this, it is solid and resistant.

Recommended for use on: wooden ship and aeroplane bodies, diorama scenery, all kinds of woodwork and carpentered installations, and any kind of construction where lightness is of the essence.

Sold as Follows

Blocks: These are what are called laths in carpentry. The standard sections are these (millimetres):

20 x 20	20 x 40	40 x 50
20 x 30	20 x 50	40 x 80

Standard length: 1 metre

Blocks should be used for basic construction work like timbers and planks in real building. Can be worked with a saw or an X-Acto tool.

Dowels: Two standard shapes are available—square or rectangular. The standard sections are:

2 x 2	3 x 15	5 x 15
2 x 5	4 x 4	6 x 6
2 x 10	5 x 5	8 x 8
3 x 3	5 x 10	10 x 10

Dowels can be used for all kinds of jobs on boats, aeroplanes, dioramas, electric trains etc.

Sheets: The standard thicknesses of balsa are graded in tenths of a millimetre. There are two widths, 80mm and 100mm; lengths, 1m and 1.35m. Thicknesses available:

5/10	15/10	50/10
6/10	20/10	100/10 (10mm)
8/10	30/10	150/10
10/10 (1mm)	40/10	200/10

In the choice of materials, sheets of 100/10 allow joints to be made with blocks upwards of 20mm thick.

Special Shapes
Particularly supplied for aeroplane construction. Half-round: length 100 x 8 and 10mm along side.

Trapezoid sections available:

15 x 5mm	20 x 5mm	25 x 6mm

(These woods are generally supplied coloured right through)

Triangular sections available:

8 x 8	10 x 10	12 x 12

Balsa timbers:

50 x 90	70 x 90	70 x 100
90 x 90	100 x 100	70 x 120

Large balsa laths:

20 x 20	50 x 50
30 x 30	70 x 70

Mahogany: These days the name mahogany is used, often wrongly, to sell all red-wood trees of equatorial origin. These woods have the following technical qualities: good hardness, the right amount of flexibility, excellent resistance to mechanical working and good tolerance of hygrometric variations (that is, atmospheric humidity).

Its use is recommended for basic construction work where weight is not a factor, but where solidity may be essential (e.g. electric trains, fixed and solid models, solid scenery etc.).

Sold as Follows
Blocks: Two standard thicknesses available, 20/10 and 30/10. We must also include mahogany used for decoration, which comes in wood veneer 5/10 thick.

Dowels: When purchasing, care must be taken to see that the dowels are uniform; in no case must they show propellor-type marks or be badly worked on one side. Mahogany dowels, rectangular or square, come in the following dimensions:

2 x 2	2 x 8	3 x 7
2 x 3	2 x 10	3 x 12
2 x 5	3 x 5	5 x 5
2 x 6	3 x 6	

Poplar: For the model-maker, poplar is counted among the hard woods. It is used as something in between mahogany and balsa. For small components, it is good for lathe-work: it can be used to make supporting structures, struts and braces. It is used also in making the basic structures of buildings, boats, vehicles and dioramas.

Sold as Follows
Sheets: Two standard widths, 80 and 100mm, in thicknesses graded by tenths of a millimetre.

10/10	20/10	40/10
15/10	30/10	50/10

Dowels: Two standard shapes, square or rectangular:

1.5 x 1.5	2 x 10	5 x 5
1.5 x 5	2 x 15	6 x 6
1.5 x 10	3 x 3	8 x 8
2 x 2	4 x 4	10 x 10

Round poplar dowels are also available, and the model-maker will find them useful. They come in the following diameters:

3, 4, 5, 6, 8, 10 and 15mm.

Birchwood: An ingredient of plywoods used in making large-scale models of aeroplanes and boats. Recommended for all models exposed to the elements (all models taken outdoors).

Sold as Follows

It comes in planks of standard shape: 210 x 420—but also 310 x 620 and 1,250 x 620. Standard thicknesses: 3, 4, 5 and 7mm. Birchwood veneer is also available in the following thicknesses: 3, 4, 5 and 7mm.

Limewood: Sold in fine-quality boards. Particularly useful for building aeroplanes and ships.

Sold as Follows

Widths from 100 to 300mm, length 850mm, thicknesses 4, 6, 8 and 10mm.

Beech-wood: Used in making the sealed plywoods used for aeroplanes and ships. It is also available in sheets of veneer and in round dowels.

Sold as Follows

Veneer: thicknesses of 0.8, 1, 1.2, 1.5 and 2mm.
Plywood: 3 and 5mm, in numerous shapes.
Round dowels: length 1m, diameters graded by millimetre from 2 to 20mm.
Grooved dowels: these are square-section dowels with one or two grooves. 16 x 12 and 4 x 4mm, length 1 metre.

Other Woods

The woods which we have added below are really of secondary significance, but they sometimes have a part to play in building scenery or the making of certain details.

Willow: Very supple material, available in 2, 3, 4 and 5mm diameters; permits the making of curved structures.

Cork-oak bark: Used essentially to reproduce rocks and cliffs in dioramas and electric train systems. It can be obtained at florists' accessory shops.

Cork: Often used in interior decoration, it is available in various forms in do-it-yourself shops; in 4−5mm thick boards, in thin sheets 0.8 to 10mm thick, or in bricks and blocks. It allows very accurate reproduction of a stony appearance or road surfacings. Broken into small pieces, cork allows the imitation of blocks of stone in some kinds of scenery.

Box-wood: Difficult to find these days, box-wood is excellent for lathe-work. It allows very exact working of parts. Only useful for the model-maker who wishes to make highly individual models.

Paper and Cardboard

These materials, which the model-maker will use extensively, are most often available in artists' supply shops and decorating shops but, here again, it is one's own creative imagination that will determine their different uses.

Drawing paper: The most highly recommended is that which comes in packets measuring 297 x 420 or 210 x 297. Always select 224mg/m^2. This is the only weight that will stand up to being worked with after painting. The uses of drawing paper are innumerable: conversions of models, flooring, roofing, special components, backdrops etc.

This material stands up well to water-colour paints, acrylic paints and special plastic paints, but it does not stand up well to spray paint. Packs of coloured drawing paper save a lot of time when making certain things, without any loss of quality.

Kraft paper: Better-known under the name of wrapping paper. Good for use as backing, but also when you need to reproduce planking or certain kinds of roofing. An economical backdrop or moulding base.

Card and scraperboard: These materials are used by artists and professional model-makers. They are expensive. They have one or both sides satin-finished or glazed, black or white, mounted on a thickness of card of about 1.5 to 2.5mm. They must be cut with a trimmer. Openings or windows to be made must be cut with a strong knife. Use not recommended for beginners.
 Uses: buildings facades, stations, roads, bridges etc., and all stationary scenery that will be painted with water-colours.

Plastic Products

These articles are generally available only at shops catering for professional model-makers, which are rather few and far between. However, it is a good idea to know of their existence.

Sections and angles: These items, in principle intended for the model-maker making models for property developers and architects, come in the following dimensions:

I-Sections: Length 610mm.
Section: 3.2 x 1.9, 4.8 x 2.4

U-Sections: Length 380mm.
Section: 3.2 x 1.2, 4.8 x 1.6

T-Sections: Length 380mm
Section: 3.2 x 3.2, 4.8 x 4.8

Angles: Length 380mm.
Section: 2.4 x 2.4, 3.2 x 3.2, 4.8 x 4.8

There are also extra-long sections in the shape of a barrier or safety-railing. It is obvious that all these sections allow the construction of metal-looking constructions (ships, buildings etc.), and can be fixed by simple glueing.

Transparent plexiglass: This rather costly material allows the construction of windows and frames, and the protection of tableaux. It comes in 15/10, 20/10, 30/10 and 40/10 thicknesses. It is available in sheets measuring 800 x 600mm and 1,600 x 1,200mm.

Rhodoid: In a similar material, rhodoid, one can obtain sheets consisting of small plastic hemi-spherical shapes. Used in window-dressing and in jewellery, these hemispheres can be of great service to the model-maker in the following cases: bombardier's or cockpit canopies, roofing of a modern building or of science-fiction scenery, protection of delicate models etc. Each sheet contains 30 hemi-spheres with diameters varying from 10 to 50mm.

Altuglass: Altuglass hemispheres are widely used for showing off better certain items in exhibitions and in display-cases. They can be used equally well to protect delicate tableaux and models. Available in diameters ranging from 100mm to 600mm. Very expensive.

Cellulose acetobutyrate (CAB): Sheets of blue or green-tinted plastic. For putting coloured glass etc. into buildings, ships and aeroplanes, but can also be used to give coloured background effect. Standard sizes sold: 500 x 300mm in sheets, 0.75 and 1.5mm thick.

Celluloid: Transparent sheets for all kinds of use, easy to glue. Especially good for making all kinds of glass (cabins, cock-pits, windows of all kinds). Beware, this material is highly inflammable. Standard thicknesses 0.25 and 0.5mm.

Polystyrene: A basic model making material, this can also be obtained in standard sheets. Available in the shops in 23 x 23cm sheets, thicknesses 25/100, 50/100, 75/100 and 100/100. Polystyrene also comes in 'mini-strips', little strips designed for fine work.

Metals

As in industry, metals come in standard shapes. Three basic metals in model making: aluminium, brass, steel. For the shapes and dimensions given here, we are talking of minimum standard production sizes, which means that you can sometimes find intermediary dimensions as well.

Aluminium: This is the softest of the metals, and the lightest too. When it is being machine-worked, the machine itself, drill or lathe, must work at high speed. It is a metal that fouls up machines, but can be sawn, drilled or planed without the slightest difficulty. If it is not treated with a special protective varnish, it tarnishes with age. Aluminium is the basic material of complex mechanical models. It can be used to make frames and chassis (cars, boats, buildings).

Sold as Follows
Metals come in standard 1 metre lengths. Tubes: external diameters graded by millimetre (20/10, 30/10, 40/10, 50/10, 60/10 and 100/10).
Foil: comes in small sheets of metal 50cm wide, available in thicknesses 5/100, 10/100, 20/100 and 40/100.

Brass: This is a fine-looking, malleable alloy, lending itself to all sorts of coach-work (cars), boiler-making (locomotives) and allowing conversions and modifications of existing models. Can be worked as easily as aluminium: drilling, planing, polishing, hammer-beating and stretching without problem. Used in all kinds of scale-models, depending on the shape chosen.

Sold as Follows
Tubes: Available in 20/10, 30/10, 40/10, 50/10, 60/10, 70/10.
Rods and wires: 5/10, 10/10, 15/10, 20/10, 25/10, 30/10.
Solid square sections: 2 x 2, 3 x 3, 4 x 4, 5 x 5, 10 x 10.

Hollow square sections: 4 x 4, 5 x 5.
Angle-irons: 2 x 2, 3 x 3, 3 x 6, 4 x 2, 5 x 5, 6 x 6, 7 x 7 (dimensions indicate length of each wing of the angle-iron).
U-Sections: 2 x 2, 3 x 3, 4 x 4, 5 x 5, 7 x 7, 8 x 8 (all with squared corners).
T-Sections: 2 x 2, 4 x 4, 6 x 6, 8 x 8.
I-Sections: 4 x 2, 5 x 2.5, 8 x 4, 10 x 5, 12 x 6.
Bars: This is the name given to a sort of rather thick and rather wide metal dowel. Available in 1mm thickness, widths 20 and 60mm.
Railway-line: Specialist model railway suppliers sell rail-shaped sections on the HO, O and I scales for the construction of railway lines to scale.
Foil: Sheets available in 50cm width, in the following thicknesses: 5/100, 10/100, 20/100, 40/100.

Copper: People often confuse copper and brass. Brass is mistakenly known as 'yellow copper', as opposed to natural copper, which is known as 'red copper'. This material has all the characteristics of brass. Easy to work, it is very malleable. It is expensive, and not found in all modellers' supply shops. It is often better to obtain it from do-it-yourself shops. Copper foil comes in small sheets 30cm wide in the following thicknesses: 10/100 and 15/100. One can also sometimes use fine copper wire, available from radio and electrical equipment shops.

Steel: Difficult to work, being a rather hard metal, it is available in modellers' supply shops almost exclusively in the form of threaded rods in standard diameters, or again in the form of thick wire known as 'piano wire', in the following dimensions: 5/10, 10/10, 15/10, 25/10, 30/10.

Special Materials

These are products which are available in the shops, but which one does not normally think of in connection with making models.

Wood 'micro-veneers': A number of woods, including oak, teak, birch-wood and citron-wood, come as extremely thin veneers on a silk paper backing measuring 65 x 50cm. Can be used to obtain a wooden look on very small models of things like houses, furniture, boats, carts etc.

Metalflex: This is an adhesive laminate, metalled on one side. It is only 0.06mm thick. Comes in various finishes: copper, aluminium, chrome etc. Ideal for reproducing these metals on small flat or slightly curved surfaces—fuselages, coachwork, buildings.

Transfer sheets: Known in the printing world and other areas as Letraset and Letter Press, these black transfer sheets reproduce a variety of designs over large areas: stones, bricks, paving stones, tiles, wood etc. All you have to do is to stick the sheet to the paper or cardboard surface, cut around the contours and press the design on. Allows flat but suggestive reproduction of materials. The sheets come in a 32 x 42cm format.

Adhesive mesh strips: As useful to the model-maker as a tube of glue. These are coloured strips, matt or glossy, sold on spools in all colours—silver, gold, red, yellow, green etc. They come in widths 0.4, 0.79, 1.59, 2.38, 3.17, 4.76, 6.35, 12.7 and 25.4mm. Mesh strips sold under the name Normatape allow the lateral decoration of aeroplanes, cars, ships, locomotives and carriages to give a grainy painted effect. Application is very easy, and is often better than brush-painting.

Embossed sheets: In plastic or in cardboard, these sheets reproduce rocks, paving, bricks, and tile or slate roofing very realistically. The sheets are coloured throughout. Available at modellers' supply shops, they can all be simply glued on. Indispensable for accuracy in country-side scenery and buildings.